Who Is the Devil?

Nicolas Corte

Who Is the Devil?

SOPHIA INSTITUTE PRESS
Manchester, New Hampshire

Who Is the Devil? is an English translation by D. K. Pryce of *Satan l'adversaire* (F. Brouty, J. Fayard et Cie., 1956). The English translation was originally published simultaneously in 1958 by Hawthorn Books, Inc., New York, and McClelland and Stewart, Ltd., Toronto, as volume 21 of the *Twentieth Century Encyclopedia of Catholicism*. This 2013 edition by Sophia Institute Press includes minor editorial revisions to the 1958 translation. Scriptural quotations are taken from the Knox Bible.

Printed in the United States of America

Cover design by Carolyn McKinney

Sophia Institute Press
Box 5284, Manchester, NH 03108
1-800-888-9344

www.SophiaInstitute.com

Nihil obstat: Johannes M. T. Barton, S.T.D., L.S.S., *Censor Deputatus*
Imprimatur: E. Morrogh Bernard, *Vicarius Generalis*
Westmonasterii, June 26, 1958

Library of Congress Cataloging-in-Publication Data

Cristiani, Léon, 1879-1971.

[Satan, l'adversaire. English]

Who is the Devil? / Nicolas Corte.

pages cm

Originally published: New York : Hawthorn Books, 1958, in series: The twentieth century encyclopedia of Catholicism ; v. 21. Section 2, The basic truths.

Includes bibliographical references (pages).

ISBN 978-1-933184-88-3 (pbk. : alk. paper) 1. Devil—Christianity. I. Title.

BT982.C7513 2013

235'.4—dc23

2012050793

First printing

Contents

Who Is the Devil?

Chapter 1

The Fall of the Angels

If you ask a theologian the question that forms the subject of this book, "Who is Satan?", he will doubtless answer, "Satan is the commander-in-chief of the fallen angels." A commander-in-chief implies an army, a hierarchy, a body of troops.

What do we mean by angels?[1] Are angels persons like human beings, with a body and soul, or have they a more ethereal constitution than ours? Are they pure spirits, that is, without a body? In that case, what is meant by *fallen* in the theologian's definition of Satan?

First of all, however, we must ask ourselves if we are really concerned here with authentic theology. Has the Church any teaching on the subject of the angels and Satan? Is the Christian, careful to believe everything that the Church believes and teaches in God's name, obliged to believe in the existence of the angels and Satan? Or is he allowed to consign the whole

[1] For this subject, see Pie-Raymond Regamey, *What Is an Angel?*, vol. 47 of the *Twentieth Century Encyclopedia of Catholicism* (New York: Hawthorn Books, 1960).

subject to the indeterminate domain of tradition, legend, or Christian folklore?

It would not be particularly surprising to encounter, even among enlightened Christians, those with doubts on the whole matter, people who prefer never to raise the question of the existence of angels and devils, lest they be obliged to come to a decision about it.

Yet that is obviously a kind of defeatism, a petty spiritual cowardice, or at least theological laziness. We must face problems boldly and come to reasonable, sound conclusions about them. And that is precisely what this little book endeavors to do for the general Catholic public and even for the public taken in its wider sense.

∞

> God is the Creator of all things visible and invisible, spiritual and corporeal, and by His almighty power, from nothing, at the beginning of time, He made both creatures, the spiritual and the corporeal, that is, the angels and the world. Then He made the human creature, composed of a spirit and a body combined.

This definition is a dogmatic one, which all Christians are obliged to accept. All must subscribe to it not only outwardly but inwardly, by a genuine act of faith. It emanates from the fourth Lateran Council in 1215 and was directly aimed at the Catharist or Albigensian heresy, about which we shall have more to say later. This heresy, which wrought great havoc in France and Italy, taught dualism—that is, a system according to which two principles are in opposition for all time: God and matter, good and evil.

If we identify Satan with evil, we must then entirely abandon any attempt to make Satan a sort of independent and eternal rival to God. Satan—if he exists—can only be one of God's creatures.

But we need not go right back to the Middle Ages to discover a dogmatic definition on this point. Much more recently the Vatican Council of 1870 returned to the Lateran formula and fixed it in its definitive form, which reads as follows:

> This God, the one true God, in His goodness and by His almighty power, not that He may increase His beatitude, nor that He may gain thereby, but to manifest His perfection by the blessings He bestows upon His creatures, has made out of nothing, by a sovereign act of free will, at the beginning of time, both the one and the other creature at the same time, the spiritual and the corporeal: that is to say, the angels and the world. Then He made the human creature composed of a spirit and a body together.

From these solemn official pronouncements it follows that the existence of the angels and their creation by God are dogmas of the Catholic Faith, and we may not question them.

If we took literally the definitions given by the Lateran and Vatican councils, we would have to admit that the creation of the angels is contemporaneous with that of the visible world of which the earth forms a part.

There is nothing to prevent the creation of the angels being connected with that of the material universe, and it even contains an interesting idea, for it provides, if we dare use the expression, spectators and witnesses, endowed with intelligence and capable of love—or hatred—to that immense revelation of the omnipotent creative power.

But let us hasten to say that in the Vatican council's definitions, the words "at the same time" are not meant to oblige us to believe in this simultaneity of time. All that emerges from the formulas is that the creation of the angels took place before that of men. If the angels were created at the same time as what has been called "the primitive atom," eight thousand million years ago, they are of much longer standing in time than we.

Definitions given by the Church are always necessarily based upon divine revelations. Our Scriptures, which are inspired by God, must therefore contain exact and formal declarations concerning angels and devils—the fallen angels. In fact, Holy Writ is full of definite evidence on this matter. The angels were concerned in all the great events of our religious history. Their mysterious intervention—whose different modes we shall have to study—is directed sometimes in our favor and sometimes against us. Thus, even before our history begins, we find that angels are already divided into two categories: beneficent or good angels and maleficent or bad angels. There were guardian angels, angels of temptation, angels of retribution, and accusing angels. We shall see in the next chapter that it was a bad angel who took the form of the serpent to lead the first woman astray. It was an angel, a good one in this case, who guarded the entrance to the lost paradise and caused to shine, as a warning, before our first forefathers after their fall, "a sword of fire that turned this way and that" (Gen. 3:24).

From then onward, angels occur very frequently in Scripture. Remember the angels of Abraham, of Agar in the desert, and those seen by Jacob in his famous dream, all the way up the ladder that rose from the earth to Heaven. We shall also have to speak of the intervention of Satan in the story of Job; and there is no need to mention the apparition of angels related in the book of Tobit or in the prophets.

Nor was it only under the Old Law that the angels, whether good or evil, exerted their influence upon the chain of human events. The Gospel also speaks to us about them. The archangel Gabriel appears first to Zechariah and then to Mary, the immaculate Virgin. Joseph is visited in his sleep by angels. They appear before the shepherds of Bethlehem, heralding the birth of Jesus and singing a canticle whose words are both simple and profound: "Glory to God in high Heaven and peace on earth to men that are God's friends!" Naturally, the Church adopted these words, expanding them into the paraphrase we say or sing at Mass: *Gloria in excelsis Deo!*

At a later stage we shall have to consider Christ's temptation in the wilderness. We know that, once temptation had been triumphantly repelled by Him, "angels drew near to serve him" (cf. Matt. 4:11).

We need go no further, for it would be necessary at this stage to summarize our entire book. Every page of it will in fact offer proofs of the very real existence of Satan and the fallen angels, or devils, and of their continual intervention in, and close connection with, the story of mankind.

We are now in a position to state one first conclusion: in all that the Scriptures tell us about angels, good and bad, it is impossible to see mere metaphors or poetic expressions and personifications. And so St. Paul, wishing to give us a glimpse of the splendor of the Son of God, writes:

> He is the true likeness of the God we cannot see; his is that first birth which precedes every act of creation.

> Yes, in him all created things took their being, heavenly and earthly, visible and invisible; what are thrones and dominions, what are princedoms and powers? They were all created through him and in him. (Col. 1:15–16)

The apostle thus sets before us the vast unity of creation, visible and invisible. It must be admitted that such a dogma enlarges immeasurably our normal horizon. For angels do exist! That means that the ladder of beings, that ladder seen by Jacob in a prophetic dream, extends from the lowest form of creatures right up to those nearest to God. Our world contains, within the framework of inorganic beings that serves as a pedestal for all the rest, swarms of living forms—about three hundred thousand vegetable species and more than five hundred thousand animal species that have emerged from the Creator's hand as from an inexhaustible fountain. And above our world, in which man holds ever greater sway over nature, with its countless riches and incalculable energies, revelation shows us another domain even richer, more wonderful and diverse. It is the domain of the spirits; it is the infinite variety of invisible essences, of subsistent, thinking, and loving substances.

Let unbelievers enclose themselves within their narrow thoughts and limit their vision to this small world that we can see, to this brief life that is but a preamble to our immortality. They sometimes say that religion "narrows" the mind! We answer them with the grandiose vision that faith unfolds before us. The man who has never left his village believes, as they do, that the world ends at the summit of the mountains he can see from the top of his church tower! But the soul that, by faith, has let itself be taught by God prefers to probe into the mystery of God's works. The earth is so small and the heavens so vast!

What could be more natural than to admit that between the human race and God's throne there is a great multitude of pure spirits, of ardent thoughts, with intuitions as vivid as lightning and as big as the stars, spirits endowed as we are—and better than we—with intelligence, will, and liberty, capable, in consequence, of obedience and love or of revolt in hatred, and so playing a role far superior to ours in that gigantic struggle between good and evil which forms the central drama, the *raison d'être* of creation!

Having once reached this first conclusion, we inevitably arrive at the problem of the fall of the angels.

Who is Satan? That is the question before us. Satan was an angel, one of the most beautiful, the most intelligent, the most powerful and the most "willful," by which is meant most capable, according to his choice, of love or hatred. Principally, *Satan* means the drama of the fall. It is this that we must try to understand.

∞

When we speculate about the nature and constitution of the stars, when scientists send artificial satellites far above our globe to pick up cosmic rays, what we are trying to grasp is the physical unity of the universe. Increasingly we believe that this unity exists and that the most distant galaxies are not composed of elements different from those that we know on earth.

Now, all the scriptural data and the theological conclusions drawn from them allow us to argue in exactly the same way concerning the moral and religious unity of spiritual creation. This is indeed noteworthy. The unity of God is reflected in all His works. The material universe is established in the unity both of its elements and of the laws that govern them. The invisible universe, of souls and angels, is likewise founded upon the unity of the laws that govern spirits, intelligences, wills, and hearts. We human beings are spirits bound up in matter. That is no less a mystery than that of pure spirits. But we both have the same laws, the same duties; we tend toward the same end and by analogous means.

This similarity between human souls and angels was clearly stated by Christ when he said that "those who are found worthy to attain that other world and resurrection from the dead will be as the angels in heaven are, children of God now that the resurrection has given them birth" (Luke 20:35–36).

In his description of Heaven, the great seer in the book of Revelation, St. John, portrays it as a medley of angels and of the righteous from our earth. And in his letter to the Hebrews St. Paul's vision is the same.

We are thus entitled to suppose that it was with the angels as it is with men. The great point to consider here is freedom. But why freedom? Because without it there is no personality. The creation of free beings is God's triumph. He could do nothing greater or more beautiful. But is liberty an end in itself? No, it is only a means, the means of asserting one's personality. In its turn, is personality an end in itself? Yes and no. Yes, because we are created only to develop all the possibilities of being that are in us. No, because our possibilities of being cannot be isolated from the essential Being, who is God. Here it is a matter of metaphysical necessity.

The laws governing spirits are not arbitrary. They derive from the essence of things. God is the Being. Being and good are coextensive; they are two words meaning the same thing. But good is "self-diffusive," as an old axiom of philosophy says, meaning that good is love. If this is so, it is only by loving that a created being can make real all the potentialities that are in him. When Jesus said: "You shall love the Lord your God with all your soul, with all your heart, with all your strength, that is the first and greatest commandment," He was formulating not a somewhat artificial, superficial, extrinsic requirement but, rather, a metaphysical necessity compelling recognition from all spirits, whatever their nature.

In this way the gift of freedom can be understood. Those who, like Luther and Calvin, dared to speak of slave-will[2] in connection with man have totally misunderstood the divine plan. If love is the first law given to spirits, freedom is necessary to them because love under compulsion is a contradiction in terms and is no less absurd than a square circle. It was necessary for the angels to be free, as it was for Adam and Eve, and as it is for us to be free to choose our own course—that is, to give our love to God or to refuse to do so. The whole spiritual drama of the world is contained in this cry of anguish from Francis of Assisi: "The beloved is not loved!" The mystics have said that in every possible tone, and no Christian should be unaware of it.

Liberty forms the great hazard run by spirits. Everything depends upon the use they make of it now or in the future.

The fall of the angels becomes in this way as intelligible to us as the fall of Adam or our own fall. Lamartine speaks of *La Chute d'un Ange* ("The Fall of an Angel"). It is not only a poetic invention; it is an everyday reality, the very basis of existence on earth. It was, too, the crucial point in the life of the angels: The unity of laws of the spiritual world.[3] This unity is no less

[2] Cf. Martin Luther, *De Servo Arbitrio*.

[3] For the problems of grace, see Henri Daniel-Rops, *The Theology of Grace*, vol. 23 of the *Twentieth Century Encyclopedia of Catholicism* (New York: Hawthorn Books, 1960).

logical and necessary than the physical unity of the material universe.

The fact, and it is moreover a certainty, of the fall of a considerable number of angels, transformed by their sin into bad angels, that is, into devils, is our warrant that celestial beatitude was granted to pure spirits only after a trial of love similar to, or even identical with, that which is imposed upon us.

Thus, we hold, so to speak, both ends of the chain, and that is enough to enable us to outline the moral and religious laws of the world of angels. Like us, they were created good, capable of obedience and love, made for the goodness and happiness that metaphysically they could find only in God. But also like us, they were endowed with liberty, because without liberty no love is possible in the true meaning of the word. And thus, they were capable of falling. In fact, it is only in God that liberty is identified with good. Everywhere else liberty is not by itself good, but only the faculty of seeking and attaining it. This suggests that it is also the faculty of turning aside from and betraying it.

Destined, as we are, to a supernatural end, which is the Beatific Vision of God, the angels must have been raised to what is called the supernatural state by a free gift that we usually term *sanctifying grace*. Our theological virtues of faith, hope, and charity possessed their counterparts in the angels in the dispositions and possibilities with which God had endowed them.

How long did this first form of existence last? We do not know. There are even well-founded reasons for saying that we cannot situate the angels in time without detriment to their nature. They are above time. No more need be said about this lest we stray into hazardous speculation.

What is certain—and by no means conjectural—is that like us, the angels underwent a test, and we have explained why. There is no happiness without love, there is no love without freedom, and there is no freedom without a choice—that is to say, without a test. By bearing these equations in mind we are led to the very depths of the mystery of our own destiny.

In what did the trial of the angels consist? How long did it last? These two questions remain unanswered for us. Our Scriptures, which are our only source of accurate knowledge on the matter, are silent upon both points.

What they do say, however, is that in the first place there was a fearsome battle between the angels. And there again we find such a close analogy with what happens among human beings that we are obliged to infer the unity of the moral laws in the spiritual world.

If we open the book of Revelation, the most extraordinary book in the Bible, we shall find many incomprehensible things in it. But here and there, on almost every page a clear light shines through. In the twelfth chapter we read:

> Fierce war broke out in heaven, where Michael and his angels fought against the dragon. The dragon and his angels fought on their part, but could not win the day, or stand their ground in heaven any longer; the great dragon, serpent of the primal age, was flung down to earth; he whom we call the devil, or Satan, the whole world's seducer, flung down to earth, and his angels with him. Then I heard a voice crying aloud in heaven: The time has come; now we are saved and made strong, our God reigns, and power belongs to Christ, his anointed; the accuser of our brethren is overthrown. Day and night he stood accusing them in God's presence; but because of the Lamb's blood and because of the truth to which

> they bore witness, they triumphed over him, holding their lives cheap till death overtook them. Rejoice over it, heaven, and all you that dwell in heaven; but woe to you, earth and sea, now that the devil has come down upon you, full of malice, because he knows how brief is the time given to him. (Apoc. [Rev.] 12:7–12)

That is one of the most grandiose frescoes ever painted for the mind of man. Nor is that all. This battle of the angels had an object, a stake, a purpose. What were they fighting for in such a world, so different from ours? Enough has been said to make it clear that it could only be a matter of love or hatred. The Scriptures, in a context entirely different from that of the book of Revelation but consistent with it, cast unexpected light on the subject. We are told: "Pride is hateful before God and men.... Of all sin pride is the root. Leave it, or a tempest of blasphemy shall follow, and thou thyself be ruined at the last" (Ecclus. 10:7, 13–14 [RSV = Sir. 10:7, 13]).

Pride is at the origin of all rebellion. Pride is preeminently a sin of the spirit. Pure spirits, like angels, could not sin, as men do, through sensuality but they could very easily sin through pride.

The idea of their own perfection, the power of their intelligence, and the grandiose visions it offered them could all lead them into the temptation to pride, through self-satisfaction. You may say: how inconsistent, how blind, how foolish! But is not that just what we constantly see all around us and in ourselves? Doubtless, the author of Ecclesiasticus cannot say to Satan what he says to man about pride: "How can that which is earth and dust be puffed up with pride? He who, even in his lifetime, has his entrails already filled with rottenness?" But what is incomprehensible for us, of so little account and wretched as we are, would be less so for the angels. In any case, it seems quite clear that the sin committed by Satan and his angels could only be a sin of pride! This sin was doubtless the wish "to become God himself," at least in the eyes of the angels who desired to follow him and whom he managed to lead astray. To wish to become God is the height of pride. It is the crime that, among human beings, the false messiahs of philosophy and politics commit with varying degrees of enlightenment and violence. The denial of God is the supreme act of pride. It is also the denial of love, the essential revolt, the unforgivable sin.

Unforgivable we have said, and there is another mystery that we must endeavor to penetrate. The sin of the angels was not forgiven. That is a fact. Whatever Origen,[4] seventeen centuries ago, and in our day, Papini,[5] may have thought about it, if the angels' sin was not forgiven, it is because it is unforgivable in itself, for God's goodness is so great that, if the sin were not unforgivable by nature, He would have found a way of forgiving it. St. Augustine clearly saw that: "Since we know," he wrote, "that the Creator of all good sent no grace of atonement to the bad angels, how can we fail to conclude that their sin was judged all the more culpable because their nature was sublime?"[6]

Theologians have carefully examined this problem. The explanation of it, according to them, is that the nature of the angelic spirit is to see in a flash the reasons both for and against before making its choice and never again, metaphysically, to be

[4] Origen (c. 185–c. 254), Greek Christian writer, teacher, and mystic.

[5] Giovanni Papini (1881–1956), Italian journalist, critic, poet, and novelist.

[6] St. Augustine, *Commentaries on St. John*, in *Patrologia Latina* 35, col. 1924 (hereafter quoted as Migne, *PL*).

able to retract once that choice is made. The angelic intelligence is intuitive. It operates by powerful inspirations. It never returns to things seen, once they have been seen, nor, consequently, reconsiders decisions once taken. That means that an angel is incapable of repentance. Sin regretted is a sin that can be forgiven. But a sin not followed by repentance and retraction is an unforgivable sin.

That is the case with the sin that we call final impenitence. Once it has left the body, the human soul becomes fixed in its state. It is subject to the laws applying to pure spirits. For the soul of the righteous and the faithful angels can no longer desire to retract their love, nor can the damned and the devils retract their hatred.

∞

One point at least remains to be dealt with, and that is the possibility of a battle between the angels, of some leading the others astray, of the formation of two sides—the faithful and the rebels. Here again we are reduced to conjecture, but once more we can appeal to the unity of the laws of the spiritual world.

Like us, the angels operate by a "spiritual impulse," what we call an intention. It is an everyday fact that we address God by prayer. But what counts in prayer is not the words, but the "intention"; it is that "silent music," as St. John of the Cross says, which gives our prayer its real value. Likewise, when we try to communicate by prayer with the Blessed Virgin, with a saint, or even with one of our loved ones who has died, to achieve this, we do not rely on words or on the sound of the voice, and not even on the words we whisper in our hearts. We rely on our intention.

Here, of course, we take cognizance of the data—very vague and uncertain, it is true—offered by psychical science. In any case, it is certain that there do exist, even among ourselves on this earth and in this life, mysterious methods of transmitting thought that would probably be far easier and better understood if we were trained to do it. But this thought-transmission, hindered and obscured as it is in current practice by the noise and bustle of the material world, is simply the normal means of exchanging desires and feelings in the world of pure spirits. So by his powerful will, Satan, who was still an angel of light—Lucifer—could both challenge the faithful spirits commanded by Michael, whose name is descriptive—"Who is like God?"—and also rally to his cause all those who, answering his call and following his example, chose the revolt of pride and, against all logic and justice, desired to make themselves gods.

All that the Scriptures tell us of the pride of the devils, their relentless struggle against the kingdom of God, and the battle fought between Michael and Satan gives the impression of some immense tragedy on the grand scale, in comparison with which our own conflicts seem petty and unimportant; we see a gigantic tussle between the angels, a division into two "rival blocs," as we would say on earth, but also a brilliant victory for love over hatred and for obedience over pride, owing to a decisive intervention by divine justice that gave to the faithful angels the victory and the reward they deserved, but which pronounced a sentence of irrevocable damnation on the rebels.

For the fallen angels, as for us, there existed therefore a moral order that should, and could, have been a source of dignity, beauty, and eternal beatitude for those adhering to it, but which would punish the rebels by a sort of degradation and decadence, leaving them with the aptitudes inherent in their nature, but dedicating them to evil, so satisfying God's justice.

Thus, from one end of the spirit universe to the other, a majestic unity appears, a grandiose harmony and a rigorous logic of laws and golden rules that govern all existence. We can only feel growing within us respect and love for the very basis of moral life and the essential principles of religion, when we see it thus translated to a superior world and compelling recognition by creatures so far above us, with that same inviolable rigor that our consciences are bound to acknowledge them to possess.

Chapter 2

The Tempter and the Accuser

The creation of the angels, the trial to which they were put, and the fall of a great number of them in Satan's wake might all have belonged to a world so foreign to our own that we knew hardly anything about it. Our thoughts are often directed toward other globes, inhabited perhaps like ours but by other human species similar to our own, perhaps superior or inferior, but about which so far we know nothing. The same might easily have applied to angels and devils. And it is doubtless in a very close relationship to this physical unity of the material universe and to this moral unity of the spirit universe that human beings should consider the intervention of the angels and the devils in our own history. God likes to link up together each and every part of His work. He has created an interdependence between the stages of creation. The vegetables feed on the minerals, the animals on the vegetables, and men feed on both. Everything holds together in nature. And the observation that has just been made on the relationship between living beings and food is only one very crude aspect of the countless bonds existing between all creatures.

It is not surprising, therefore, that God should have bound the world of angels to that of human souls. If other inhabited planets do exist, a day will doubtless come when the connection between them and the earth is established in its turn. In the case of angels and demons, it was an accomplished fact right at the outset.

What use could the Creator make of the fallen angels in relation to us? An old Christian proverb said: "The Devil carries stone." That means that the Devil himself can serve God's purposes. The use that God makes of him can be called "the art of taking good from evil" (St. Augustine). If he was banished from Heaven, he was not banished from creation. By God's will an important part remains for him to play in it.

This part is precisely the one that Satan had played in the great battle of the angels. It is inherent in the logic of his being. In his revolt he seduced a number of angels, and he will try to seduce the greatest possible number of souls in this same rebellion. In a word, and by the very choice that he had freely made long before the first man was created, he will be the Tempter.

John Henry Newman said that our certainties concerning faith, what he called "the grammar of assent," are derived much more from a convergence of proofs, from a harmony between laws and things, than from one single rigid piece of reasoning. The role devolving upon the Devil in the history of mankind is simply one of these convergences and harmonies. It was right that these free beings, endowed with intelligence and love, that God, by giving them a reasoning soul, had just drawn from the animal stage of evolution or, if it is preferred, from the clay of the earth, should be put to the great trial of love just like the angels. It has been explained in the previous chapter why this trial is necessary. For a free creature, happiness is happiness only when it is merited, for it is only at this price that it properly belongs to him who won it in the hard fight. Thus, humanity required a trial befitting its strength, just as the angels did; and it was in this connection that Satan was used by God, for it is impossible to suppose that he could tempt Adam and Eve without God's permission. This temptation formed part of the divine plan, the whole magnificence of which Satan did not realize. He could have no notion that the day would come when his victory over Adam and Eve would cause to be sung in Christ's Church that astonishingly audacious *felix culpa*.[7] He was following his bent, he was obeying his nature, by becoming the Tempter. But the word *temptation*, which to us in our weakness means something sinister, really only signifies a putting to the test, that is, a trial. As this trial was necessary, it offered, if we may use the expression, a ready-made opportunity for Satan.

In the battle, moreover, the "good angels" were to have their part to play, but this time on our side, as friends, protectors, and as we say, guardians. In fact the world of angels and devils is even more closely bound up with the world of souls than is the world of vegetables, animals, and minerals with that of human bodies, which is saying a great deal.

We can now leave generalities and consider the facts known by biblical revelation. We shall find there, at every turn, new harmonies and convergences in Newman's sense of the words.

∞

The first human couple had been placed by God in an enchanting place that we call earthly paradise. In spite of all its

[7] "O happy fault": "O happy fault, O necessary sin of Adam, which gained for us so great a Redeemer!" (St. Augustine).

delights, and by virtue of the law of spirits, Eden was necessarily a battlefield, for in it was to occur the meeting of the two parts of the spiritual universe: that already existing—angels and devils—and that which had just appeared on the little earthly planet. By the war between the angels the struggle begun between good and evil and, as St. Augustine was to say later, between the City of God and the City of the Devil, was transported to our globe.

It is very probable that the trial imposed upon Adam and Eve was something far more difficult than those that we have to face. We are the "sons of sin." Our first parents had just come from God's hand. In them the very perfection of humanity, as it is described by Catholic theology, gave to their trial a more grandiose and formidable character. The destiny of mankind was in their hands. The light that God made to shine within their conscience, by a kind of infused knowledge, that they received at birth, the complete harmony that existed between their faculties, the entire subordination of the flesh to the spirit, in their nature, did not allow their obedience or their revolt to be commonplace.

In a fine thesis in the *Summa Theologica*,[8] St. Thomas Aquinas—and a number of great theologians have followed him in this—has established that Adam and Eve were incapable of committing a merely venial sin. And that gives us—and should give us—an exalted idea of the strength of their souls endowed by God with the supernatural and preternatural gifts of which the theologians speak. Venial sin is a somewhat crude inconsistency. For our first forefathers, there was only one possible trial, which we might call: For or Against, or even All or Nothing.

[8] St. Thomas Aquinas, *Summa Theologica*, I-II, Q. 89, art. 3.

What does it matter after that if the biblical story of the Fall should be put before us in a popular form and even with obviously mythical elements? It is the substance of things that we must look for. And that is what Bossuet expressed in decisive terms in the following passage:

> "Of all the beasts which the Lord God had made, there was none which could match the serpent in cunning." Here in the apparent weakness of so strange a beginning to the story of our misfortunes, lies the admirable depth of Christian theology. Everything appears to be weak; we venture to say that everything in it seems to wear a fabulous appearance; a serpent speaks; a woman listens; a man so perfect, so enlightened allows himself to be led astray by a crude temptation; the whole human race falls with him into sin and death; it all appears senseless. But it is here that the truth of this sublime saying of St. Paul's begins: "That which is in God [apparent] folly, is wiser than the wisdom of men; that which is in God [apparent] weakness, is stronger than the strength of all men."[9]

We shall not try to deprive the biblical story of the almost naive simplicity that constitutes its charm. We freely admit that there is allegory in it, a presentation designed to appeal to the imagination and, perhaps, features of popular history. But we must go to the heart of the matter. Satan—for it is indeed he, and the book of Revelation clearly denounced him when speaking of the dragon—appears to the first woman in visible form.

[9] Jacques-Bénigne Bossuet, *Élévations à Dieu sur les mystères*, sixth week, first *élévation*.

Did she see him with the eyes of her body or with the eyes of her soul? The point need not be discussed. What is certain is that Satan, somehow or other, spoke to Eve. "He attacks us"—it is again Bossuet speaking—"at our weakest point." It is what he is going to say that matters to us. Thus, we are to see what he thinks and so, doubtless, obtain a glimpse of the "diabolical psychology." At this point it would be fitting for us to consider the convergences and harmonies that Newman sought in all things.

Now, there are three stages in the dialogue between Satan and the first woman, three stages that summarize the whole of his strategy as the Tempter, three stages that are exactly those that we all know in this perpetual drama of temptation which is something so profoundly human.

First stage: a simple question, asked as if out of kindly curiosity with apparent indifference, almost in a friendly way: "What is this command God has given you, not to eat the fruit of any tree in the garden?" Here, it is simply a matter of opening a conversation, of insinuating a doubt, if possible, of setting in motion what we should call the spirit of criticism. With this innocent-seeming question the Tempter is already questioning a principle. He appears to invite investigation of God's command, its limitations and merits. Remotely he is inducing a frame of mind in which the woman will call in question the law laid down for her and the authority imposing it.

And these tactics succeed. The woman enters into conversation. She answers the Tempter: "We can eat the fruit of any tree in the garden except the tree in the middle of it; it is this God has forbidden us to eat or even to touch, on pain of death."

Second stage: This reply is sufficient for Satan to judge that the woman is wavering, that she is held back only by fear and not by love. If this is so, she is on the point of falling. Satan himself knows quite well that true obedience is that of love and not of fear. At once he changes his tone. He no longer interrogates as if he did not know and required information. He becomes more friendly still, more pressing. He seems to pose as a liberator. From insinuated doubt he goes on to a categorical denial.

"Now," he says to the woman, "what is this talk of death? You shall not die." Not at all! *Nequaquam!* There is a distinctive trait of satanic psychology: Satan is the supreme denier and might indeed be defined as the Denier, or what amounts to the same thing, the Liar.

Nor does he rest there. He goes much further and reveals the very depths of his perversion by his next remark. He must cast the most insulting suspicion on God himself; he must dazzle the woman's mind with his own mad dream that caused his downfall. Indeed, what profundity there is in what he now says (third stage): "God knows well that as soon as you eat this fruit, your eyes will be opened and you yourselves will be like gods, knowing good and evil!"

Thus, it is not enough for him to have substituted the most shameless denial for the most subtle doubt. He makes of God a jealous and distrustful being. If God has forbidden the fruit to be eaten, it is because He is afraid of rivals. He wishes to keep us in a state of dependence. He wishes us to be slaves, not children!

"You will be like gods!" Such is the diabolical psychology. To make oneself God shall be for men as for angels the very depth of sin. "Who is like God?" Michael, the chief of the faithful angels, had replied. It is about God, his nature, his love, and participation in his divinity that the battle is fought. Jesus also was to promise His followers to become "gods," to be, in the words of St. Peter, "sharers in the divine nature" (2 Pet. 1:4), or according to the words of St. John: "We shall be like him!" (1 John 3:2). And with all their soul the mystics were to seek to immerse themselves so completely in God that they were but one with him. Enraptured, Paul was to say exactly the same thing: "I live no more; but it is Jesus who lives in me!" (Gal. 2:20).

It is obvious that in the seemingly "fabulous" story of Genesis there is an almost unfathomable depth of meaning. And such are the harmonies and convergences that it proffers that we cannot ask for anything better.

Is it not Satan's sophism for all time when he says to Eve: "You will be like God, knowing good and evil"? To possess all the light, you must also possess all the darkness! To "know life," you must have abused it! To attain truth, you must have experienced error.

What happened then in the soul of the mother of men? The most alluring temptation does not deprive us of our freedom; it was even truer of our first forefathers than of the fallen, diminished beings that we have become through their disobedience. Jesus was to show later on—and we shall have occasion to mention it—how we must answer Satan. But Genesis says: "The woman, who saw that the fruit was good to eat, saw, too, how it was pleasant to look at and, charmed the eye, took some fruit from the tree and ate it; and she gave some to her husband, and he ate with her" (Gen. 3:1–6).

The sin was consummated, a sin of the spirit more than of the flesh. Satan had played an incalculable part in it. He had, so to speak, obsessed them with this thought, which had been the inspiration of his revolt: "You will be like God; you will be gods, knowing good and evil!"

This disordered ambition and the outright disobedience that it provoked constitute a sin similar to that of Satan himself. However obscured our own conscience, it is impossible for us not to realize its gravity.

The punishment was not slow in coming. Its effects are still evident in us. On the part of infinite Love it has provoked its counterpart.

After the fall in Adam came the restoration in Jesus Christ. The holiness of the "Son of Man" answered the sin of the "father of man." The temptation by Satan in the earthly paradise is therefore one of the most significant factors in the whole of our spiritual history, the first act of the great drama we are still living, and in which each one of us in turn must choose one side or the other.

In the following dogmatic definition, the Council of Trent has clearly emphasized that part of the story of Genesis which must be retained in our faith:

> Let him be anathema who does not admit that the first man, Adam, after having transgressed God's commandment, in the earthly paradise, immediately lost his holiness and the justice in which it had been established, and incurred, by committing such an offense, the wrath and indignation of God and subsequently death, with which God had previously threatened him, and with death, captivity under the dominion of him who, from that instant ever after, had dominion over death, that is to say, the Devil, and that Adam, by committing this offense, suffered a fall both in his body and his soul.[10]

[10] Council of Trent, decree of June 17, 1546, session 5, canon 1.

The whole Christian religion proclaims that that was anything but a fable, a tissue of allegories, or a myth. Satan was an actual reality, a living and thinking being, a personality. And there are few personalities who have exerted a stronger influence on our destiny. Later on, Jesus was to say to His enemies: "You belong to your father, that is, the devil, and are eager to gratify the appetites which are your father's. He, from the first, was a murderer; and as for truth, he has never taken his stand upon that; there is no truth in him. When he utters falsehood, he is only uttering what is natural to him; he is all false, and it was he who gave falsehood its birth" (John 8:44).

A murderer from the first: such is the first definition of Satan. It is he, literally, who put us to death, who introduced death into the history of mankind. And the tragedy is that because he said to us: "No, you shall not die!" that we do die.

He is therefore a murderer because he is the father of lies. Such is the answer given by the facts to the question asked in this book: Who is Satan? This problem has been constantly before us. Satan is the author of death because he is the author of lies. To measure the satanical reality, that is, the role Satan plays in our history, we would have to be able to measure the immensity of three things: concupiscence and sin, lying, and death. All who consider it will realize that Satan is the great protagonist in the human adventure. And all that remains for us to say will be only a confirmation of this first statement.

Before going further, we should recall this saying of Ecclesiasticus in a context dealing with good and evil originating in woman: "Through a woman sin first began; such fault was hers, we all must die for it" (Ecclus. 25:33 [RSV = Sir. 25:24]). But if Eve had her responsibility in this drama, Satan's was far heavier.

"God, to be sure," says the book of Wisdom, "framed man for an immortal destiny, the created image of his own endless being; but, since the devil's envy brought death into the world, they make him their model that take him for their master" (Wisd. 2:23–24).

If we have rather stressed this first appearance of Satan in the history of mankind, it is because it is the prelude to all his age-long activity among men. Without exaggeration it could be said that he is the accomplice if not the direct inspirer of all human crimes, from that of Cain down to those of our own time, and the instigator, as we shall have to show, of all that is evil and, as we say so glibly, "infernal" in our civilizations!

Yet he was also, as we shall show, an opportunity for moral victories on the part of the saints, as clearly emerges from that magnificent poem the book of Job. Few books in the Bible present more magnificent images or deal with more human problems: the problem of the trial, the problem of suffering, the origin of evil, the greatness of God, the sovereign justice that is in Him. What is the Gospel, if not the drama of the suffering of the Righteous One, the drama of the Cross? And yet, before that, the book of Job had already told of the suffering of the righteous.

But if suffering is one of the aspects of evil on earth, it is obvious that Satan must have a word to say in this. In fact, he appears to us in the book of Job as one of the authors of suffering. God permits it. Satan inflicts it with God's permission. He inflicts it to drive man to despair and to blasphemy, while God permits it to test the degree of our faith, our confidence, our fidelity and love.

Doubtless, in the book of Job, as in Genesis, there is also an affabulation, which it is wise to interpret with care and a certain breadth of mind. We must look for the substance as in the wonderful account of the temptation.

> One day, when the heavenly powers stood waiting upon the Lord's presence, and among them, man's Enemy, the Lord asked him where he had been. "Roaming about the earth," said he, "to and fro about the earth." "Why then," the Lord said, "thou hast seen a servant of mine called Job. Here is a true man, an honest man, none like him on earth; ever he fears his God and keeps far from wrongdoing." "Job fears his God," the Enemy answered, "and loses nothing by it. Sheltered his life by thy protection, sheltered his home, his property; thy blessing on all he undertakes; worldly goods that still go on increasing; he loses nothing. One little touch of thy hand, assailing all that wealth of his! Then see how he will turn and blaspheme thee." (Job 1:6–11)

We know what follows. *Satan* means "the adversary," or even "the accuser." It is a role that bears a very close relationship to that of tempter, a role in which we know that Satan was a past master.

But there is more than one feature that we should consider in the book of Job as a whole. First, Satan's place in creation. Clearly he keeps to himself. The "heavenly powers" are the angels. God has no need to ask them in order to know where they have come from. It is He who sends them, and they are simply His faithful messengers. Without doubt, in His infallible knowledge, He knows very well where Satan comes from also, but His way of interrogating Him is aimed at making us understand that Satan takes his own course, with God's permission; in a word, that he does what he wants to do, although within the limits fixed by Providence. The book of Job permits us to define these limits. It is only by God's permission that Satan is able to bring down all sorts of catastrophes upon everything belonging to Job, reducing him to the last stages of misery. And when, in spite of everything, Job says: "The Lord gave, the Lord has taken away, blessed be the name of the Lord!" (Job 1:21), Satan urges God to allow him to go further still.

"'Skin must suffer before skin grieves!'" he says brutally and cynically. "'Nothing a man owns, but he will part with it to keep his skin whole. That hand of thine, let it fall on bone of his, flesh of his; see if he does not turn and blaspheme thee.' And thereupon said the Lord to man's Enemy, 'Have what power over him thou wilt, so his life be kept safe in him'" (Job 2:4–6).

Then the trial is revealed in all its violence. Job is smitten in his body and in his flesh. And it is without doubt Satan again who causes his wife to curse him, then his best friends to accuse him, for they are determined to proclaim him guilty and to dishonor him simply because he is wretched. In their eyes one cannot be wretched and innocent at the same time. That raises the problem of the suffering of the just, as we have said, in all its bitterness. We solve it nowadays by the contemplation of Christ's Cross and by association with this Cross, which is a pledge of future glory. But Job belongs to the Old Testament. He cannot know this answer, which is the only complete one. He has, it seems, the greater merit for not abandoning his pure monotheism, his deep filial piety toward the Creator and the power of his hope in Him. The book of Job is but a stage in the revelation of the ways of God, but a stage admirably described and handled. The magnificence of the world in which God has established us should suffice to reveal to us His sovereign wisdom and consequently to lead us to perfect submission and to a total surrender into His hands.

Job's victory is an example of the triumphs man can win over Satan's malice. He is far from always emerging victorious. He was conquered the first time by Michael and his angels. He was defeated, at least according to what was written in the book of Job, if we suppose that the figure of Job never really existed. But it is hard to believe that the author of the book did not have a model in his mind, if not before his eyes. He is defeated, above all, by Jesus Christ as we shall describe in the next chapter. And he will be conquered, according to the book of Revelation, at the end of time.

Some points remain to be considered before we leave the Old Testament.

In the first place, the Devil is represented in it as a creature of God and by no means as an independent and rival principle to God. St. Gregory the Great, commenting on the prelude to the book of Job, asks himself how Satan could have presented himself at the court of the King of Heaven, with the angels. And he answers his own question by saying that if Satan lost the beatitude of Heaven he nevertheless kept his nature, which was like that of the angels.[11] And that is to be the common teaching of the Fathers.

In the second place, Satan's psychology, as it emerges from the two great texts of the Old Testament examined here, is of unusual coherence. The Satan who, in the form of the serpent, spoke to Eve is exactly the same as the one who tries to lead Job to blasphemy and despair. Between his role as tempter and that of accuser there is an undeniable kinship. In both cases we have

[11] St. Gregory the Great, Migne, *PL* 75, col. 557.

a being who does not love us; who is jealous of us; who would like to drag us to destruction with him; who, to achieve his purposes, does not hesitate to lie or to inflict the most dreadful calamities upon us; in short, someone who revels in doing harm to us: a murderer from the first, the father of lies, whom Jesus Christ denounced.

That such a figure is constantly at work among men is what helps to explain why the history of mankind should be so full of troubles, disturbance, unrest, and bloodshed and most of the time so inhuman. If one of the ancients has seen fit to say that no wild animal has shown itself to be more ferocious than man, it is largely true because of Satan's action among men. Whatever else we may have to say concerning him will only strengthen us in this conviction.

Chapter 3

Satan and Jesus Christ

If, in Newman's sense of the word, there is a striking convergence in the religious history of the world, it is to be found in the decisive role played by Satan both in the fall of Adam and Eve and in the life and death of Jesus Christ.

One of the most realistic ways of understanding the life of Jesus, and even more His death, is to look upon it as a tremendous battle fought by Satan against the Savior of men. We are not accustomed to considering it from that angle, and yet it is thus that the tragic grandeur of the Christian drama appears most clearly to us. He who had been a "murderer" from the first, Satan, reached the very peak of his triumphs with Jesus, for with Jesus he achieved deicide. He never aspired to anything greater. He was satisfied.

But his triumph rebounded upon himself. We detect, in his deicidal madness, the same error that we notice nowadays in that triumph of technique and science, the atomic bomb. This victory of the human mind, puffed up with pride, is also its downfall. Man's knowledge rebounds upon man. He draws back in horror from his own power. In the same way, the death of Christ, the supreme exploit of Satan's hatred, was the signal for his defeat and the decline of his dominion.

By saying that, are we yielding to a theological illusion? Are we the victims of groundless speculation? Which evangelist, the authorized witness of Christ's works and of the profound reason for the Incarnation of the Word, shall answer these questions on our behalf? The other evangelists took their point of departure in time but one alone, John, looked to eternity: "At the beginning of time the Word already was; and God had the Word abiding with him, and the Word was God.... And the Word was made flesh and came to dwell among us!" (John 1:1, 14).

Now, this same St. John, wishing to tell the Christians at the end of the first century of the final reason for the Incarnation, wrote in his first letter: "If the Son of God was revealed to us, it was so that he might undo what the devil had done" (1 John 3:8). And from beginning to end of the same letter, he identifies sin with the work of the Devil. For him, all sins committed since the beginning of the world have been at the instigation of the Devil. If Cain killed his brother, it is because he "took his character from the evil one" (1 John 3:12). The whole Christian problem consists in eschewing the evil one, escaping from the grasp of the evil one, of belonging only to God. And so St. John's conclusion is as follows: "The man who has been born of God, we may be sure, keeps clear of sin; that divine origin protects him, and the evil one cannot touch him. And we can be sure that we are God's children, though the whole world about us lies in the power of evil" (1 John 5:18).

It is Jesus that St. John means by this vivid expression: the man who has been born of God. And in the passage you have just read, Jesus' mission is once again summarized: He came "to undo what the devil had done."

∞

If we now open the other Gospels we may be surprised to find, right at the outset, the mysterious picture of a great struggle between Jesus and Satan in the wilderness. It is called the Temptation of Jesus. John, faithful to his method, which consisted in completing the story told by his predecessors, approving by his very silence what they had so admirably said already, does not speak of this "temptation." And yet he must have known about it. Evidently he had heard of it from the same source as the other Evangelists, from Jesus in person. Just think about it: Christ's temptation in the wilderness had had no witnesses. It is almost certain that it could not have had any. So if the three synoptic Gospels speak of it, practically in the same terms, it is because Jesus desired to speak to the Apostles about it Himself and that He had insisted upon it so as to make them understand that it had been one of the important features of His messianic life. The Evangelists placed it, as did God Himself, at the very beginning of Christ's public life, before any preaching of the gospel, immediately after His baptism in the Jordan by John the Baptist and after the proclamation of which Christ's baptism had been the occasion: "This is my beloved Son in whom I am well pleased!" (Matt. 3:17).

Not only is it very remarkable that it should be Jesus Himself who instructed His Apostles about what happened in the wilderness on this occasion, but the expressions He used to tell of the "temptation" also require our attention. It is true that St. Matthew and St. Luke simply say that Jesus "was led" into the wilderness "by the Spirit," expressly "to be tempted by the Devil." And that in itself is suggestive. But "the evangelist St. Mark, the sublimest of all abbreviators," as Bossuet said, is much more forcible here. He shows Jesus not only "led" into the wilderness, but Bossuet, unable to translate the word he uses, writes: "According to St. Mark, He [Jesus] was thrown, carried off, driven there."

Was it therefore so necessary that Jesus should be tempted by Satan? If, as we have said, the purpose of the Incarnation is none other than to "destroy the works of the Devil," that is, to change the course of the religious and moral history of mankind, can we not see how necessary this first encounter was? What happened is exactly the opposite of what had happened in the earthly paradise. Instead of a "garden of delight," we are in a wilderness. Instead of the gentle animals that we can picture to ourselves in Eden standing around Adam and Eve when they gave them their names, Jesus will be, as St. Mark says, "with the wild beasts."

Instead of appearing in the form of a serpent—if something more than allegory is to be seen in this detail—Satan seems to have shown himself to Christ as he really is, either as an infernal spirit or in human shape. The new Adam was therefore obliged to face the same adversary as did the primitive Adam.

In our accounts of the temptation there are two characters: the Son of Man and Satan. It was without any doubt the most terrible duel the world has ever known. There can be no greater mistake than to minimize, however little, such an episode. We are in the presence of one of those events dominating the ages which fits into the gigantic struggle between good and evil, between love and hatred. Of this struggle we have so far recalled the most salient features: the battle between Lucifer and Michael, between the good angels and the devils, the casting off of the rebels, the temptation of Eve and Adam in the garden of Eden.

The temptation of Christ in the wilderness is the prelude to the persecutions of which Christ was the object at the hands of His enemies and consequently of His death on the Cross. They did not hesitate to term Him "a votary of Beelzebub" (Matt. 12:24)—one of Satan's names; in itself that is indicative of the diabolical psychology, for this insane accusation is worthy of the father of lies.

What happened then, probably in January or February of the year 28, in the wilderness of Judah, not far from the Jordan, was the revenge of humanity, represented by the new Adam over the devil who had conquered the old Adam. By recounting it to His Apostles afterward, Jesus surely wished to stress the fact that the whole of his life was to be a struggle with, and victory over, Satan.

∞

If we understand St. Mark's text aright, the temptation of Christ lasted forty days. So it must not be reduced to the three particular assaults that are related by St. Matthew and St. Luke. There were forty days of penance, fasting, and prayer on the part of Jesus and forty days of attacks, insidious whisperings, subtle suggestions, and perfidious insinuations on the part of Satan. We may perhaps, as Christ did when relating them, divide into three categories, so to speak, the temptations by the evil one upon the mind of Jesus.

In the Garden of Eden, Satan took as the point of departure for his "temptation" the fact that God had forbidden Adam and Eve even to "touch" a certain tree. Satan's tactics are logical. He bases his argument upon a fact, a fact known to the one who is being tempted, an important fact that should occupy his mind. He does likewise here: he begins with the event which had just taken place on the shores of Jordan, the proclamation of the Son of God that had been heard there.

"If thou art the Son of God": these are Satan's first words. Doubtless he has no desire to hint at any denial of this point. He seems to admit the thing as a possibility. Nor does he try to go too deeply into the manner of Christ's filiation with God. The angels were called "sons of God" in the book of Job. For Satan, Jesus is perhaps something like that, a "son of God" in the sense that the angels are, or that we ourselves become, by virtue of our baptism. That is of little importance, but it is by commencing with this title that Satan is going to "tempt" Jesus.

He waits until Jesus is hungry, as a result of the superhuman fast that He has imposed upon Himself. Eve yielded to the bait of a fruit that was "pleasant to look at," appetizing, and desirable. In this wilderness, Satan has nothing like that to show to the hungering Christ. No matter! There are stones to be found there that look very much like loaves of bread. The ancient pilgrims of the Holy Land have named them *judaic stones, lapis judaicus*. Satan ventures a subtle temptation: "If thou art the Son of God, bid this stone turn into a loaf of bread." What is his purpose?

"It is a strange temptation," said Bossuet, "to try to persuade the Savior to show Himself to be the Son of God and give proof of His power simply to satisfy the tastes and needs of the flesh. Let us understand by that that it is also the most powerful bait in the world: he attacks us through the senses, he studies the dispositions of our bodies and makes us fall into the trap. Such, then, is the first temptation, that of sensuality."[12]

[12] Bossuet, *Élévations à Dieu sur les mystères*, twenty-third week, third *élévation*.

We might also say that Satan wishes to perform a miracle by the agency of Jesus, but a miracle that will be performed *suadente diabolo*, a miracle inspired by the Devil. In itself, the miracle asked for was or could be legitimate. Jesus did not hesitate, in the course of his public life, to feed crowds of four or five thousand people in the wilderness by means of the miracle of the loaves. What Satan asks of Him, therefore, is not beyond His power. But it is not merely a question of doing good; He must still eliminate from His action, good though it otherwise may be, any evil circumstance. Jesus unmasked the subtlety of Satan's insinuation. The demon wishes to make Him act as would a magician who has a superior power at his disposal. Above all he wants Jesus to obey him, without any consideration for the divine will. But it is this consideration alone that counts with Christ. And that is the sublime sense of His reply to Satan: "Man cannot live by bread only; there is life for him in all the words that come from God!"[13] It was tantamount to saying: there is only one necessity: the will of God. Everything else, even bodily life itself, is subordinate!

Satan, repulsed, does not lose heart. He does not give way thus easily in the temptations with which he attacks us. He resumes the conversation, beginning with that confidence in God which Jesus has just invoked. There is a close link between the second temptation and the first. He has transported Christ—either in spirit or bodily—to the pinnacle of the Temple, and he shows Him the throng of devout Jews coming up for morning prayer. What a wonderful opportunity to inaugurate a mission as a great prophet—Jesus is at least that in the eyes of

[13] Matt. 4:4. Jesus said, "It is written." He is alluding to Deut. 8:3, interpreting it freely.

Satan—by proving that He is the Son of God by means of a majestic descent, "volplaning" down, as we would say nowadays, and landing in the midst of the priests of the sanctuary and the faithful of the Law!

"If thou be the Son of God": Satan is still making an appeal to the title Jesus received by the river Jordan, a sort of invitation to the logic of things, rather as the "brothers of Jesus" were to do later on, when they still did not believe in him. When you are the Son of God, you show it! You prove it!

"If thou be the son of God, cast thyself down: for it is written, He shall give his angels charge concerning thee: and they will hold thee up with their hands, lest thou shouldst chance to trip on a stone!"[14]

Jesus had sought help from the Scriptures. The Devil shows that he is quite capable of doing likewise. But there again he fails to appreciate the character of Him whom he wishes to lead astray. For Jesus—and He was to repeat it—there is only one thing that counts: the will of God. Anything outside this will is simply a "temptation of God," that is, an abominable abuse of this word "come from the mouth of God," concerning which Jesus has just said that it is by that alone that man must live!

So he rejects abruptly Satan's suggestion: "It is written, Thou shalt not put the Lord thy God to the proof!" That is, you shall not impose your will upon Him; you shall not force His hand.

[14] A popular legend said that the Messiah would show himself at the top of the Temple roof. For this detail see Albert Frank-Duquesne, *Satan* (Paris: Desclée de Brouwer, 1948), 232. We have followed closely the interesting essay entitled "Réflexions sur Satan en marge de la tradition judéo-chrétienne," pp. 179–315; this paper is omitted from the English translation of the book (London and New York, Sheed and Ward, 1951).

It is tempting God if you try to "drive Him into a corner" or to demand a miracle of Him that He has not promised or that does not form part of His plan. In the same way, later on, the Jews demanded from Jesus "a sign from heaven." And He rejected their request. Of course, miracles have a role to play in the history of revealed religion. There is no faith without miracles, but they obey a mysterious law laid down by God alone.

In the face of this determined submission to God alone, Satan seems to lose patience. In any case he pretends no longer. He takes his all. He transports Christ—physically or spiritually—to a high mountain. He displays before Him the immensity of his kingdom. Everything is his, everything belongs to him. He is truly the "prince of this world" (John 12:31). But all of that he holds in contempt, provided he can obtain the submission and homage of this "Son of God" who has just refuted him twice running. "Once more," says St. Matthew, "the Devil took him to the top of an exceedingly high mountain from which he shewed him all the kingdoms of the world and the glory of them; and said, I will give thee all these if thou wilt fall down and worship me!" (Matt. 4:9).

What pride in this proposal! And how well it comes into line with the psychology of the Devil as we have depicted it so far in this book! And what a revelation for us! How blind we have been, in our history, not to have seen that it is Satan who "leads the dance," that it is Satan whom most of those we name "great men" have obeyed rather than God. The thirst for conquest, human ambition in all its forms, the desire to dominate, to rule, even if to do so it is necessary to "fall down and worship Satan"—that is, to violate the divine law—is not that the very substance of universal history, from the very beginning right up to the present time?

Did not the messianism of the Jews, in the time of Christ, and all the false messianisms that followed, right up to the present time, lead, in one way or another toward the possession of all the kingdoms of the earth, even if it were Satan who gave them?

In this story of the temptation of Christ, we are therefore in the very midst of humanity, in the very stuff of which history is made.

How will Christ answer? Between him and Satan all men will henceforth have to choose! Let us listen to His command: "Then," says St. Matthew, "Jesus said to him, Away with thee, Satan: for it is written, Thou shalt worship the Lord thy God, and serve none but him!" (Matt. 4:10).

This time Jesus commands as the master. He brings to an end a conversation that has lasted long enough. He tells us also not to fear the so-called "omnipotence" of Satan. It is to be noticed that He does not deny this apparent "omnipotence." On the contrary, He will have occasion to confirm it when He calls Satan the prince of this world, and he does so three times in the Gospel according to St. John. But it is a "principality" that He does not accept, that He rejects, and that He has come to fight and to destroy.

∞

It is not therefore from the lips of Jesus that we shall find words expressing doubt concerning Satan's power or, as we see nowadays, concerning his very existence. If Christian tradition was right to make the expression "gospel truth" synonymous with "the absolute truth," nobody can doubt that Satan existed and still exists, nor that his power in the world is enormous, nor that everything that the genius of man has invented for the purpose of killing, from Cain's cudgel to the hydrogen bomb, is a product of Hell. Satan is a "murderer" from the first, says Jesus. Everything that leads to murder is therefore in his province. A book has been published on "Satan and the present day." If what we have just said is true of Satan, it is undeniable that Satan has never been more active than in the present time, for never have the means of killing been more numerous, more efficient, more monstrous, or more truly diabolical.[15] And we should not forget that vice kills more people than war, and that vice has always existed on our planet and that it was particularly prevalent at the time when Jesus came to wage war on Satan.

Yet was St. John right to attribute the purpose of the Incarnation to this alone: "to undo what the devil had done"? It is to Jesus that we shall look for an answer.

We have just said that three times He uses this striking expression "the prince of this world" when referring to Satan. The first time is when He has just entered within the Temple walls on the eve of His supreme Sacrifice. "The time has come now," he cries, "for the Son of Man to achieve his glory. Believe me when I tell you this; a grain of wheat must fall into the ground and die, or else it remains nothing more than a grain of wheat; but if it dies, then it yields rich fruit.... Sentence is now being passed on this world: now is the time when the prince of this world is to be cast out. Yes, if only I am lifted up from the earth, I will attract all men to myself!" (John 12:23–24, 31–32).

Doubtless, all men will not respond to this "attraction," but it will not be any less real, and in any case there will be, on

[15] See L. Christiani, *L'Actualité du Satan* (Paris, Editions du Centurion, 1954).

earth, those "ten just men" (Gen. 17:32) who would have sufficed to save Sodom and Gomorrah.

The second time, Jesus is even more explicit and invites us to penetrate the mystery of His own death. He says to His disciples after the Last Supper, "I have no longer much time for converse with you; one is coming who has power over the world, but no hold over me. No, but the world must be convinced that I love the Father, and act only as the Father has commanded me to act!" (John 14:30–31).

These are strong words. They treat Satan as someone who might have "rights." He certainly has, up to a certain point, of course, over the rest of men, because willful sin has made them the slaves of Satan. But over Jesus he has no rights. And precisely because of that, Satan will be thwarted in his malignant plans. Having no rights over Christ, he will have him put to death by the iniquitous judges and by the relentless executioners who will serve as his instruments. And this death will be the end—theoretically—of his reign. In a sense too, it will be the real end of his reign, because he will have involuntarily contributed to paying to God, through the death of Christ, the most magnificent homage that any creature, substantially united to the Word of God, can possibly pay to the Creator! Whether the Devil likes it or not, his crime is a source of ineffable glory for God.

A third time, Jesus calls Satan the prince of this world when he declares, in a context full of mystery for us, that "he who rules this world has had sentence passed on him already!" (John 16:2).

We shall speak of this sentence later on. But we must remain convinced by the infallible words of Christ, which are the absolute truth, that Satan is an exceedingly important figure and by no means a fiction or a childish belief. On the contrary, we shall have to say that the Devil's most infernal trick at the very time that he was wielding the greatest power within Christianity itself was to make people believe that he did not exist!

If he did not exist, it might be said that all Christ's work would be reduced to nothing, for He came only "to undo what the devil had done."

This expression moreover leads us to look more closely into the concept of Redemption.

∞

More than a century ago, in 1905, a young teacher of theology, Abbé Jean Rivière, published a book entitled *Le Dogme de la Rédemption, Essai d'étude historique*. Nine years later, in 1914, he completed his first work by a second volume: *Le Dogme de la Rédemption, étude théologique*. For many modern minds it was a source of amazement to observe how widespread among the Fathers were theories explaining the Redemption that today we would describe as naive and archaic. Abbé Rivière was the first to speak of it in this way.

In what then did his theories consist? In taking literally the word *redemption*, which means "buying back." Jesus Christ had really given His blood as the price for our souls. Just as in certain medieval legends, which are perhaps founded on a certain basis of fact, we encounter people who have made a pact with the Devil to sell him their souls and even their children's, so do we find that a certain number of the Fathers suggested and believed that, by their willful disobedience in the earthly paradise, Adam and Eve had literally sold themselves and all their posterity to the Devil. God, who always respects the liberty of His creatures, without, of course, approving of such an abominable pact, had allowed Satan to take possession of his prey, but within certain narrow limits, for human beings always remained free to reinstate themselves and master their evil tendencies. This is borne out by what is said in Genesis concerning Cain (Gen. 4:7). Nevertheless, the fact remains that Satan had acquired a hold over the sons of Adam. And Jesus, the only one who could say: "He has no hold over me!" had been charged to dispossess him of it. This dispossession was in fact the Redemption. It was admitted, therefore, that the blood of Christ had been given to Satan as a ransom to compensate him for his rights, or even that he had simply lost his rights over sinners because he had abused his power in his dealings with the innocent Christ.

A passage in John Cassian will give us an idea of the pact in question. Commenting on the words of St. Paul to the Romans (7:14) "I am a thing of flesh and blood, sold into the slavery of sin," Cassian writes:

> What sin is this? Without doubt the sin of Adam, for whose breach of faith and for whose fatal bargain and fraudulent dealings we have all been sold. Led astray indeed by the insinuations of the Serpent, he has, by eating the forbidden fruit, dragged the whole of his posterity beneath the yoke of slavery. Moreover, between seller and buyer it is customary that the one who is prepared to sell himself to an unknown owner should receive a price to compensate for his loss of liberty and for being put into servitude for life. And that is what we see has actually happened between Adam and the Serpent. He received from the Serpent the price of his liberty by eating the forbidden fruit. He forfeited thus this liberty which was his by nature and preferred to give himself into eternal

> slavery under him who paid him the mortal price for the forbidden fruit. From thenceforth he transmitted to all his posterity the new state in which he had fairly placed himself and submitted all his descendants to the same slavery under him whose slave he had become. What, in fact, can a servile marriage produce if not slaves?[16]

We have been sold therefore to the Devil! Nowadays, such a bargain is no longer comprehensible, but it was current in Cassian's day and in the preceding centuries. At any rate, Satan had power over us. And that is how original sin should be understood. Satan had become "the Prince of this world". It was by abusing his power, by pursuing his advantage from homicide to deicide, that he deserved to be dispossessed of it. And so each one of us must, by voluntarily adhering to Christ the redeemer, obtain the application to his person of the new right, namely, of belonging to God through Jesus.

∞

This dominion won by Satan over the human race should serve to explain many things for us if we could fathom the mystery of a divine justice that permitted the Devil to be used either as the tempter or the executioner of mankind. St. John declares that Satan armed Cain against his brother. But how many other Cains whose names we do not know have besmirched the history of man? "If we deny the influence of evil spirits, especially in idolatory," writes Fr. Lagrange, "we shall have to explain why ancient man was so unworthy of himself as regards religion. We shall have to explain how the tyranny of divinities, of whose

[16] [St.] John Cassian (360–433), Conf. 23, ch. 12.

existence there was no proof, could make the Carthaginians burn their own children to death and how the Greeks of the great period of Pericles could have worshipped depraved gods which they sometimes parodied on the comic stage."[17]

And also, when considering the cases of possession, which are so frequent in the stories from the Gospels, we must remember the "fraudulent" but all-too-real rights that Adam, by his sin in selling his posterity, had yielded to Satan. We shall have more to say later about possession. Here and now we can say that if there are no longer any cases of possession, it is thanks to the goodness of God and the blood of Jesus Christ. A man possessed is a sort of slave of the demon. Why are there cases of possession? Nobody can say. But it is certain that almost all the people of the world have believed in possession, and that the pagans imagined that there were men and women among them in whose bodies the false gods they worshiped lived or, at any rate, spoke and prophesied. In short, we are right to consider all these soothsayers and pythonesses as possessed of the Devil, and that is just how the Fathers of the Church consider them. But outside these cases, which were considered as normal in a pagan milieu, there were cases of possession among the Jews, and Jesus Christ had to deal with them. Not for an instant did He doubt the reality of possession. The Church, after Him, did not doubt either, and she still believes in it and can provide proofs to support it, as we shall see.

Among the Jews, possession was a well-known phenomenon, and the same remedy, namely exorcism, was used to combat it as the Church was to use on a large scale in the first

[17] Marie-Joseph Lagrange, *L'Évangile de Jésus-Christ* (Paris: Gabalda 1928), 73.

centuries of her existence, and which she was to introduce into her baptismal liturgy.

The fact that in the primitive Church there existed a special order of clergy—the exorcists—whose duty was to treat the wretched people possessed, forces us to the conclusion that cases of possession were much more frequent than they seem to be today, at any rate in Christian countries. And if that is so, we must admit that one of the benefits of the Gospel has been the very definite reduction throughout the world in the numbers of those possessed. When we have further occasion to discuss satanism and also the contemporary attitude of mind toward the subject of Satan, we shall have fresh light to throw upon this reduction in Satan's power, at least as far as possession is concerned; but it may be simply a change of tactics on the part of the Devil, the father of lies and "a murderer from the beginning."

We are not, however, obliged to believe that the number of cases of possession mentioned in our Gospels corresponds to a normal average in those times. It is very possible, and even probable, that these cases happened with unusual frequency around Jesus. The personal combination of divine and human nature in Jesus would have had as its counterpart, with divine permission, increased manifestations of diabolic power. The Incarnation of the Word was answered by Satan with diabolical incarnations of this kind, which are cases of possession. And, as is to be expected, these cases are just caricatures of the Incarnation! Much later on, the holy Curé d'Ars[18] observed that the "diabolical infestations" of which he was the object redoubled their violence whenever great sinners were about to come to

[18] St. John Vianney (1786–1859), parish priest in Ars, France.

Ars to be converted. In the domain of the occult there occur phenomena of "compensation" that have a striking analogy with what happens in the physical sphere.

But let us turn to the dominating action of Christ in cases of possession. There are abundant texts dealing with this. They say that those possessed were restored to normal, but they were not simply the sick, and that Jesus Himself made a clear distinction between disease and possession.

When Jesus sends His Apostles on a mission for the first time, He transmits His powers to them, saying: "Heal the sick, cleanse the lepers, raise the dead, cast out devils" (Matt. 10:8). The seventy-two disciples receive a similar mission.

On their return to Jesus, they relate the facts to Him and say joyfully: "Lord, even the devils are made subject to us through thy name!" And Jesus, far from reproving them for what they say, answers in tones of approval: "I saw Satan cast down like a lightning flash from heaven!" (Luke 10:17–18).

Then He described more closely the overthrow of power that was taking place. Up until then Satan had dominated the world almost as supreme master. He was indeed the prince of this world. But now Jesus could say: "I have given you power over all the power of the enemy!" But immediately afterward, to keep them in their newly found spirituality, He concluded: "But you, instead of rejoicing that the devils are made subject to you, should be rejoicing that your names are enrolled in heaven" (Luke 10:19–20).

There can be no doubt at all, therefore, about the three following points: first, it is Jesus Himself who claims an unlimited power over the devils and their chief, Satan. Second, His messianic work consists in the fall of Satan, who falls as lightning from Heaven, at the voice of His disciples, just as he had fallen from Heaven formerly, at the command of Michael and his angels. Third, He bequeaths to His disciples, that is, His Church, a power over devils that forms part of her mission on earth. In fact, when, in St. Mark, He sends forth His Apostles to conquer the world, He says to them: "Where believers go, these signs shall go with them: they will cast out devils" (Mark 16:17–18).

But apart from the general features that we have just drawn from the Gospels, we find detailed accounts of people possessed of the Devil being cured, and from them too we can learn much.

The first battle Jesus fought against possession took place in the synagogue at Capernaum, at the very beginning of His public life: "There was a man," says the text, "who was possessed by an unclean spirit, that cried out with a loud voice: Nay, why dost thou meddle with us, Jesus of Nazareth? Hast thou come to make an end of us? I recognize thee for what thou art, the Holy One of God" (Mark 1:26; Luke 4:33–35).

We should remember this example. It is extremely striking in that the Devil is forced by God to acknowledge Christ! In a special chapter we shall have occasion to report similar cases much nearer to our own times.

Now, scenes like this occurred in great numbers all around Jesus: "Many, too, had devils cast out of them, which cried aloud, Thou art the Son of God! But He rebuked them and would not have them speak because they knew that he was the Christ!" (Luke 4:41; Mark 1:34; Matt. 8:16).

The devils, therefore, feel themselves to be in a state of inferiority in the presence of Christ. They loudly proclaim their submission! One may well imagine that they do not do it willingly or in a "good spirit." The way Jesus receives their declarations is proof of that. Their faith, as St. James said, is mixed with terror: "The devils also believe and shrink from him in terror" (James 2:19).

We find this same "terror" in the well-known episode of the cleansing of the man possessed of a devil in the land of the Gadarenes. This man was uncontrollable. He tore asunder the strongest fetters. He lived among the tombs and cried out and cut himself with stones day and night. Hardly had Jesus come out of the ship when this man hastened thither and cried in a loud voice: "Why dost thou meddle with me, Jesus, Son of the most high God? I adjure thee in God's name, do not torment me!" But Jesus, treating as a stranger the poor individual lying prostrate before Him, answered: "Come out of the man, thou unclean spirit!" Thus, He was performing an exorcism very different from ours, for He spoke with authority. And for our own instruction He said: "What is thy name?"

"My name is Legion; there are many of us!" And he besought Him that He would not send them out of the country into the abyss: "Send us into the swine; let us make our lodgings there." There was in fact a great herd of swine, impure animals according to Jewish law, not far from there. And Jesus gave the devils leave and, inexplicably, the whole herd ran wildly down into the sea (Mark 5:1–20).

With this episode, how far we are from the insolent language Satan used with Christ in the desert: "Then he offered him all the kingdoms of the earth." The Devil, here called Legion—for there were many of them—humbly asks to be allowed to enter into a herd of swine! But let us not lose sight of the fact that in this case it is a mere fragment of the struggle, which began with Christ's arrival on earth, between the kingdom of God and the kingdom of Satan. It is no less important to note the features that emerge from the Gospel story concerning the action and also the psychology of the Devil.

The demons possess a penetrating intelligence and know who Jesus is. They prostrate themselves before Him unblushingly, beseeching, adjuring Him by God not to send them back to the abyss, but rather to allow them to go into the swine and take up their abode there. Hardly have they entered into the swine than, with a display of power not less surprising than their versatility, they bring about the cruel and wicked destruction of the poor beasts in which they had begged to take refuge. Craven, obsequious, powerful, malicious, versatile, and even grotesque—all these traits, here strongly marked, reappeared in varying degrees in the other Gospel narratives of the expulsion of devils.[19]

In conclusion we shall say with the same author, whose theological authority is undeniable: "The attitude of Jesus in the presence of the possessed does not allow a Catholic, nor even any attentive historian, to think that in acting and speaking as he did he was merely accommodating himself to the ignorances and prejudices of his contemporaries."[20]

Even if the cases of possession are accompanied by symptoms similar to these found in nervous or mental diseases, it is not possible to confuse them with these. In addition to the disease, in a case of possession, there is someone, there is the other one: the Devil. And doubtless one should go further and

[19] F. M. Catherinet, "Les Démoniaques dans l'Évangile" in *Satan*, *Études carmélitaines* (Paris: Desclée, 1948), 319. English translation: *Satan* (p. 168), published in 1951 in London and New York by Sheed and Ward, to whom acknowledgment is due for these quotations.

[20] Ibid., 321; English trans., 170.

say that there is a direct connection between diabolical possession or obsession and nervous disease itself. The casting out of the Devil would, in that case, lead immediately to curing the disease it had caused. Could it not be that that is a far more frequent occurrence than we realize at the present time?

Chapter 4

The Kingdom of Satan

If our interpretation of the Gospels is correct, we should find the logical development of them throughout the history of Christianity and particularly in the inspired writings of the Apostles. And so in fact we do.

The Apostles received from their Master the order to "drive out unclean spirits." We have heard St. John summarize the whole action of the Word incarnate by saying that He had come "to undo what the devil had done." The opinions of St. Paul, St. Peter, St. James, and St. Jude, that is, of all the other apostles whose writings have come down to us, are exactly the same. The most forceful is perhaps St. Paul, whose powerful genius, inspired by God, has contrasted so strongly the realm of sin with the realm of grace. Later on, when Augustine sees the whole history of the world concentrated in the struggle between the two cities, and when, after him, Ignatius of Loyola displays his famous fresco of the two standards,[21] all that both

[21] In his *Spiritual Exercises*, St. Ignatius (1491–1556), considers two standards, or banners—Christ's and the Devil's—between which Christians must choose.—Ed.

of them are doing is interpreting the thought of St. Paul. But for St. Paul, sin is not—as it is for many of us—an abstraction. The realm of sin is the realm of Satan. St. Paul seems to give the impression that sin is "someone." In our daily struggle against sin, we are struggling against Satan. It is a struggle of persons, of wills, and not simply a struggle of ideas. When St. Paul exhorts the faithful to enter the conflict, he quotes the names of people; he also sees two standards: "You must not consent to be yoke-fellows with unbelievers. What has innocence to do with lawlessness? What is there in common between light and darkness? What harmony between Christ and Belial? How can a believer throw in his lot with an infidel? How can the temple of God have any commerce with idols?" (2 Cor. 6:14–16).

It is indeed between two kingdoms that, throughout the centuries, the essential battle—the only one whose stakes are eternal—is fought. And how can we conceive the kingdom of Satan? In space the realm of Satan is our world; and in time, it is the present century.

People may perhaps be astonished that we have not said the kingdom of Satan is Hell. The point needs explanation. The kingdom of Satan is indeed Hell, but Satan received God's permission to recruit his subjects from the world. However unfamiliar one may be with the books of the New Testament, it is impossible not to have noticed how often and how strongly "the world" is condemned in them. Rarely does St. Paul mean by it material creation. In his writings, as in St. John's and even in the Gospels, when the world is mentioned, it means that section of humanity which is prey to passions darkened by religious ignorance, ravaged by vice, and finally turned aside from its essential destination, which is God. It is always in this sense that St. Paul contrasts "the wisdom of the world" with "the wisdom of God," and even sorrow according to God, or generally speaking, the things of the world with the things of God. Consequently, the world can only be the kingdom of Satan. When Jesus called Satan the prince of this world, that is just what He meant. The maxims of the world, the customs of the world, the way of living of the world all present to the eyes of Christ something satanic, and consequently they appear thus to the eyes of St. Paul and St. John. The latter expresses himself forcefully in the following passage from his first letter, and in him we hear the voice of the whole apostolic Church:

> Do not bestow your love on the world and what the world has to offer; the lover of this world has no love of the Father in him. What does the world offer? Only gratification of corrupt nature, gratification of the eye, the empty pomp of living; these things take their being from the world, not from the Father. The world and its gratifications pass away; the man who does God's will outlives them, for ever." (1 John 2:15–17)

St. Paul, as we know, is no less categorical. It might even be said that he goes further than the other inspired writers when speaking of satanic domination. St. John quotes Jesus' words when speaking of Satan as the prince of this world; St. Paul calls him "the god of this world" (2 Cor. 4:4)!

He says, in fact, in his second letter to the Corinthians: "Our gospel is a mystery, yes, but it is only a mystery to those who are on the road to perdition; those whose unbelieving minds have been blinded by the god this world worships, so that the glorious gospel of Christ, God's image, cannot reach them with the rays of its illumination" (2 Cor. 4:4). So he saw Satan struggling inch by inch against the propagation of the gospel. How could such beauty, such purity, such gentleness in Christ's gospel have failed to stir men deeply and win their hearts? But Satan is always there. He is the "god of this world" and has powerful strings to pull in the depths of human souls to prevent them from following the only doctrine of salvation that should ever shine for them. Let us make no mistake: it is a struggle here between life and death, and consequently it is a life-and-death struggle. There is nothing more bitter, more constant, more universal, or more fundamental in the whole history of mankind. This realm of death, it is Satan who is master of it. And it is again St. Paul who tells us so in this passage from the letter to the Hebrews: "And since these children"—that is, men—"have a common inheritance of flesh and blood, he too shared that inheritance with them. By his death he would depose the prince of death, that is, the devil; he would deliver those multitudes who lived all the while as slaves, made over to the fear of death" (Heb. 2:14–15).

Satan is, therefore, here on earth, he who loves death, who drives people to their death. Sin and death are his domain. The one leads to the other. Nor is it only the death of the body that interests him; it is, much more, the death of the soul. He triumphs when he has led men's spirits to the denial of the spirit. And so he gathers together all the doubters, the unbelievers, the mistrustful, those engulfed in matter, and he draws them away from the influences and from the light of the gospel, he rules over them absolutely, he becomes their god, in the strongest meaning of the word, and he is a god of darkness and lies.

∞

This intervention and presence of Satan at the very center of our conflict give to religious and moral life a particular character that is all too often not properly understood. In our textbooks of moral theology we express our meaning by abstract rules, by logical definitions, by more or less well-reasoned-out theories, by aphorisms of commonplace wisdom. These textbooks are very far removed from the reality of our actual conflict. We all tend to argue as did Socrates, the great pagan sage, according to whom it was enough to know to be able to do. All evil comes from ignorance. "He who opens a school, closes a prison." This axiom of our time is pure sophism. It is inhuman because it takes no account of man as he really is.

How much more profound is St. Paul's perception. He knows that we are "sold into the slavery of sin." We have already quoted this expression of his, which means we have been sold to the Devil by our first father. We must read the whole passage, in which he describes the moral struggle in each one of us:

> The law, as we know, is something spiritual; I am a thing of flesh and blood, sold into the slavery of sin. My own actions bewilder me; what I do is not what I wish to do, but something which I hate. Why then, if what I do is something I have no wish to do, I thereby admit that the law is worthy of all honour; meanwhile my action does not come from me, but from the sinful principle that dwells in me. Of this I am certain, that no principle of good dwells in me, that is, in my natural self; praiseworthy intentions are always ready to hand, but I cannot find my way to the performance of them; it is not the good my will prefers, but the evil my will disapproves, that I find myself doing. And if what I do is something I have not the will to do, it cannot be I that bring it about; it must be the sinful principle that dwells in me. This then

> is what I find about the law: that evil is close at my side, when my will is to do what is praiseworthy. Inwardly I applaud God's disposition, but I observe another disposition in my lower self, which raises war against the disposition of my conscience, and so I am handed over as a captive to that disposition towards sin which my lower self contains. Pitiable creature that I am, who is to set me free from a nature thus doomed to death? Nothing else than the grace of God, through Jesus Christ our Lord. (Romans 7:14–25)

In this passage the Devil's name is of course not mentioned, but anyone familiar with St. Paul's ideas knows that behind the sin, which is doubtless our own affair, there is someone who drives us to it, who rejoices in our fall, and who participates in our degradation. Sin according to St. Paul has its roots in the flesh, but it is not only against the flesh that our spirit has to struggle. Since he conquered Eve and then Adam, by means of the flesh, the demon knows that it is by that above all that he holds us and can drag us down with him in his fall.

St. Paul has strongly asserted this presence of the Devil in our moral conflicts:

> You must wear all the weapons in God's armoury, if you would find strength to resist the cunning of the devil. It is not against flesh and blood that we enter the lists; we have to do with principalities and powers, with those who have mastery of the world in these dark days, with malign influences in an order higher than ours. (Eph. 6:11–12)

There are many points to notice in a sentence so significant and so revealing. When we speak of Satan, it really does mean a person, but Satan is not alone. He has a whole hierarchy behind him. The terms St. Paul uses are the same that he uses elsewhere to mean the "choirs" of angels. And this is not surprising, for we know that Lucifer carried with him in his revolt angels belonging, doubtless, to all the rungs of the angelic ladder. All these fallen angels are "spirits of malice." There are some among them who were principalities and powers among the angels. These names inspire us with respect and should indicate possibilities of action in the universe, of which the learned men of our time give us some idea. But by their fall, the princedoms and powers in question here have not lost all their natural power, any more than one of our modern scientists would lose his knowledge and his technique by committing some moral crime. They are quite distinct things among demons as among ourselves.

Our moral conflicts, therefore, are fought not in the abstract, but against tough adversaries; and it should be added that at least we should not fear them if we do not rely on our own strength alone and that we can and must challenge them boldly in the name of our faith.

And that is just what St. Paul says when he writes: "Wear all the weapons in God's armoury," and he explains this immediately afterward (Eph. 6:14–17).

That is exactly what the chief of the Apostles, St. Peter, says in his turn, in this well-known passage from his first letter—a passage that is recited daily at Compline: "Be sober and watch well; the devil, who is your enemy, goes about roaring like a lion, to find his prey, but you, grounded in the faith, must face him boldly!" (1 Pet. 5:8–9). There again, the moral struggle is indeed a struggle against someone, a desperate struggle with the "roaring lion"!

There is nothing different to be found in St. John: read through the letters to the churches which come at the beginning of the book of Revelation and which can, moreover, be detached from it to form a separate collection. To "the angel of Smyrna," that is, the bishop of that city, John writes that he has to fight against "the synagogue of Satan." To "the angel of Pergamum," he says: "I know well in what a place thou dwellest; a place where Satan sits enthroned." In the letter to Thyatira he speaks of a sect that claims to make known "deep mysteries of Satan." He sees also in Philadelphia a "synagogue of Satan," as in Smyrna. This synagogue, in both cases, is formed of Jews who are opposed to the Gospel (Apoc. [Rev.] 2:8, 9, 13, 24; 3:9).

But all these texts, that is to say, both those from the Gospel and those that we have quoted from the apostles, seem to give rise to a question in our minds: we see Satan and his angels spread out across the earth and sky, but never in Hell. We know indeed that the devils find ways of tempting us and that, consequently, they are somehow close to us on this earth. And yet we find it almost impossible not to visualize them amid the flames of Hell. When we are told of the individual judgment to which each human being is submitted on leaving this life, we are taught that, if we have deserved Hell by final impenitence, we are immediately cast into it. A great poet Dante Alighieri, visiting Hell as a poet who is also a very learned theologian, shows us the damned being tormented by the demons. And we also have in our minds this utterance of Christ upon the last judgment: "Go far from me, you that are accursed, into that eternal fire prepared for the devil and his angels!" (Matt. 25:41).

Have the demons, therefore, the gift of ubiquity? Can they be in Hell and on earth at the same time?

Such is the problem that arises, and the answer is rather complex. When we hear the demon named Legion say to Christ: "Hast thou come here to torment us before the appointed time?" we see the beginning of a solution. It is only at the end of time, after the universal judgment, that Satan, losing his title of prince of this world—since there will no longer be a world—will be only the prince of Hell. That does not in any way mean that those who deserve to be cast into Hell by their inflexible determination to sin to the very end will not continue to be cast into Hell.

So we are right in thinking that until "the end of time" the demons prowl about over the earth. The Gospel shows them wandering through desert places, but all the time they are among us and all around us. St. Paul places them in the world, or in the darkness, or even in the lower parts of the celestial regions, all this army of beings hostile to mankind and led by Satan, who is their chief.

The exegetes think that these "lower" regions of the heavens are all sublunary, that is to say, situated between the earth and its satellite. In their estimation that is a consequence of the war that God allows to be waged, as a trial for us, between the demons and ourselves.

There is a passage in the letter to the Ephesians in which the apostle reminds the faithful of Ephesus of the time when they followed "the fashion of this world, when they owned a prince whose domain is in the lower air, that spirit whose influence is still at work among the unbelievers" (Eph. 2:2). He is obviously alluding to life in the midst of paganism. That life followed the course of this world, that is, a life of corrupt morals, hostile to Christ and His works and ignorant of the true God. But why is Satan called here "the prince whose domain is in the lower air"?

St. Paul doubtless wishes to give us to understand that the demons are lying in wait in the air all around us, ready to swoop down upon us. It is there that the "roaring lion" prowls, always ready to devour us and against whom we can defend ourselves only by faith and by watching and praying. To that we can add the words of Christ to His Apostles in the garden of Gethsemane: "Watch and pray that you enter not into temptation" (Matt. 26:41). From that we can also understand the importance that Jesus attaches to this innovation which he introduced into the sublime Our Father: "Lead us not into temptation, but deliver us from evil."

So there is for Satan and the bad angels a period of provisional remission, as far as their punishment in Hell is concerned. That does not prevent them from suffering the pain of loss, that is, deprivation of the sight of God, but this auxiliary penalty called "the pain of sense," which, with spirits as with devils, is a sort of spiritual captivity, is still only a partial one, until the end of the world.

It is perhaps in this sense that we should understand the following passage from the letter of St. Jude: "The angels, too, who left the place assigned to them, instead of keeping their due order, he [God] has imprisoned in eternal darkness, to await their judgment when the great day comes" (Jude 6).

Finally, additional light is shed upon this mystery by the text of the book of Revelation, in which St. John shows first a certain reduction in Satan's power, since the coming of Christ, then a renewal of his power of seduction, and finally the utter overthrow of his dominion:

> I saw, too, an angel come down from heaven, with the key of the abyss in his hand, and a great chain. He made prisoner of the dragon, serpent of the primal age, whom we call the devil, or Satan, and put him in bonds for a thousand years, thrusting him down into the abyss and locking him in there, and setting a seal over him. He was not to delude the world any more until the thousand years were over; then, for a short time, he is to be released....
>
> Then, when the thousand years are over, Satan will be let loose from his prison, and will go out to seduce the nations that live at the four corners of the earth.... They came up across the whole breadth of the earth, and beleaguered the encampment of the saints, and the beloved city. But God sent fire from heaven to consume them, and the devil, their seducer, was thrown into the lake of fire and brimstone, where like himself, the beast and false prophet will be tormented day and night eternally." (Apoc. [Rev.] 20:1–3, 7–10)

We need not try to see what lies beneath these tremendous images. For us their meaning is necessarily obscure. All that we can deduce from them is the certainty of the final victory of good over evil, of Christ over Satan, of love over hatred.

But we are also allowed a glimpse of the possible variations in the power of seduction of Satan and his angels, in their right to live among us and tempt us. It is certainly in anticipation of this increase in Satan's power of seduction, toward the end of time, that Leo XIII prescribed for us this formula for prayer:

> *Holy Michael, archangel, defend us in the day of battle; be our safeguard against the wickedness and snares of the devil.*

May God rebuke him, we humbly pray: and do thou, prince of the heavenly host, by the power of God thrust down to hell Satan and all wicked spirits who wander through the world for the ruin of souls. Amen.

Thrust them down to Hell! So they are not there all the time. But they "wander through the world for the ruin of souls"! That is entirely consistent with the facts given in the Scriptures as they have been related here.

Chapter 5

Do We Each Have a Personal Devil?

If we are still ignorant of a great number of laws that govern the physical world, we know still less about the laws of the spiritual world and especially those of the world of devils. And yet there is no doubt that in that world also, there are inflexible laws that the devils cannot transgress. God has never abandoned the reins of universal government. In the present chapter we shall endeavor to penetrate more closely into certain aspects of these mysterious laws.

We can consider first a passage from the Gospel that all commentators find obscure, although important:

> The unclean spirit, which has possessed a man and then goes out of him, walks about the desert looking for a resting place, and finds none; and it says, I will go back to my own dwelling, from which I came out. And it comes back, to find that dwelling empty, and swept out, and neatly set in order. Thereupon it goes away, and brings in seven other spirits more wicked than itself to bear it company, and together they enter in and settle down

> there; so that the last state of that man is worse than the first. So it shall fare with this wicked generation. (Matt. 12:43–45)

One certain conclusion we can come to in this passage is that the Devil's power of temptation has its ups and downs, that it redoubles its activity after a victory won by good over evil. Jesus doubtless wishes to forewarn us against the danger of relapses in general, but above all against the redoubled violence that Satan uses on converts. By His preaching Jesus had driven Satan back. He had shown His dominant power over devils by freeing many who were possessed. Thus Satan would make further efforts. The generation to which Jesus spoke was likely, therefore, to fall into a worse state than that which they had known beforehand, if they ignored the blessings brought to them by the coming of the Messiah. There is in fact no doubt that the position of Israel, after the coming of Christ, became much more perilous than before.

We may perhaps generalize and say that any conversion from bad to good, or from good to better, is so great an affront to Satan and his angels and the occasion of such fury that he redoubles the violence of his assaults on those who have just escaped from his clutches. It seems indeed that all converts have experienced the existence of this law. It is often after their conversion that they have had to face the most formidable spiritual trials.

∞

If that is so, we ought not to be surprised to find in the case of St. Paul himself an application of the rule that we have just stated. Among the great converts in history, there is none to be compared with him. His conversion was a real miracle of grace.

He continually reminds us of how he had sided with the persecutors of the Church and of Christ until the day he was struck down on the road to Damascus. He loudly proclaims:

> Of all the apostles, I am the least; nay, I am not fit to be called an apostle, since there was a time when I persecuted the Church of God; only by God's grace, I am what I am, and the grace he has shown me has not been without fruit; I have worked harder than all of them, or rather it was not I, but the grace of God working with me. (1 Cor. 15:9–10)

Thus we may expect to find him singled out as an object for the assaults of the Devil. And that is what he tells us:

> And indeed, for fear that these surpassing revelations should make me proud, I was given a sting to distress my outward nature, an angel of Satan sent to rebuff me. Three times it made me entreat the Lord to rid me of it; but he told me, My grace is enough for thee; my strength finds its full scope in thy weakness.... I am well content with these humiliations of mine, with the insults, the hardships, the persecutions, the times of difficulty I undergo for Christ; when I am weakest, then I am strongest of all. (2 Cor. 12:7–10)

It would be difficult to exaggerate the importance of these statements. Mystical writers have frequently emphasized the relentlessness displayed by Satan in tempting the souls of those who have advanced along the spiritual path. He tempts them in every possible way—by illness, weakness, flagrant insults, calumny, persecution, infernal invitations to impurity, and so on; the path of sanctity is not easy to tread. The higher we climb up the ladder of saintliness, the more subtle and severe are the trials we may expect to meet. That is one of the most constant laws of spiritual life. The greatest saints will find perfect peace only in Heaven.

That "angel of Satan" charged to "rebuff" St. Paul is not a rare exception. All the saints have had such a one to deal with. That is the price of holiness. The personal devil who has been driven back by grace returns to the attack and brings with him, in the words of Christ, seven—a mystical number meaning very many—spirits even more evil than he, to resume possession, if possible, of the dwelling from which he has been driven.

Is there then a personal devil, as there is a special angel, which we call a guardian angel? That is a serious question and one that was much discussed in ancient times. John Cassian quotes a passage from a book, *The Shepherd* of Hermas, that he praises highly, which, although very ancient even in his day, had retained a certain popularity. It is a curious work of the middle of the second century A.D.—between 140 and 155—and is attributed to a Christian named Hermas who is believed to have been the brother of Pius I.

This is the passage quoted by John Cassian:

> "Every man has close by him two angels, the one an angel of holiness, the other an angel of perversion." "And how then, O Lord," I said, "shall I recognize the workings of these two since they both dwell with me?" "Listen," answered he, "and you shall understand these workings: the angel of sanctity is loving and respectful, gentle and calm. So if this angel rises up within your heart, he will

> immediately speak to you of holiness, of chastity, of zeal and moderation, and of every righteous work and honest virtue. Every time these things shall rise up within your heart, you shall know that it is the angel of sanctity that is with you. Such are the works of the angel of sanctity. Confide in him and do his works. But now consider also the works of the angel of perversion. He is, above all, wrathful and bitter and wild, and his works are evil and pervert the servants of God. So every time he shall rise up within your heart you shall recognize him by his works." "How shall I recognize him, Lord," I answered, "for I do not yet know?" "Listen," he said to me. "When a surge of anger assails you, or a feeling of bitterness, you shall know that he is in you; and when also you have a desire to do many and great acts or incur needless expenditure on food and drink, and drunkenness and diverse pleasures, and the desire for women and for greed and great pride and a need to glorify yourself and everything of that sort: when you feel something of all that, you may be sure that the angel of perversion is in you. And when you have recognized his works, run from him and believe nothing he may say, for his works are evil and pernicious for the servants of God."[22]

Nowadays we should simply say that the "seven deadly sins" are the work of the Devil and that whenever we fall into one or another of them, we are in the clutches of the Devil. Now these "deadly sins" were, more or less, the law of the world before Jesus Christ, and outside of Him they still are!

[22] *The Shepherd* of Hermas; Migne, *Patrologia Graeca* 2, col. 928 (hereafter quoted as Migne, *PG*).

If we do not admit that each one of us has an "angel of persecution," just as we have a "guardian angel," the former being what St. Paul called an "angel of Satan," we are at least obliged to admit that we all carry within us the seeds of the deadly sins, and these seeds in us are the result of Original Sin, that is, they are a sort of right or hold that the Devil has over us.

∞

The Church, directly instructed by Jesus and His Apostles, clearly judged this to be the condition of any man coming to her. A mere glance at her baptismal rites will demonstrate this by reminding us how the Church envisaged the part played by the Devil in the life of an individual.

In the first place, it is highly significant that the initiatory rite that opened the door of Christ's Church was a rite of "purification," a "washing," and throughout the early centuries of the Church a real "bath" of very strong symbolical import, having the sense of a regeneration, a second birth, a total transformation of the human being. Nothing could better inculcate the idea of a previous "alienation" of this being, of a possession by the Devil. But the way in which the baptismal rite was practiced, the customs that were introduced into its ceremonies right from the beginning, the formulas that accompanied it, and the numerous preparatory exorcisms that preceded it clearly revealed the authentic thought of the Christian community on this point.

We should read, in Msgr. Duchesne's great work, the pages that he devotes to Christian initiation.[23] The only trouble, for

[23] Louis Duchesne, *Les Origines du culte chrétien* (Paris: Ernest Thorin, 1889), 292–342. Eng. trans., *Christian Worship: Its Origin and Evolution*, trans. from the 3rd French ed. by M. L.

the ordinary reader, is that he does not translate the numerous texts that he introduces; here we offer a version of at least the most eloquent of them. We shall follow his commentary step by step.

We possess numerous documents concerning Christian initiation, the oldest of which is undoubtedly our Creed, which is most commonly considered the baptismal profession of faith used in Rome.

Christian initiation comprised three essential rites: Baptism, Confirmation, and first Communion; but it is Baptism that is of more immediate interest to us. All who presented themselves were not received indiscriminately. It was by no means a mere formality, but a solemn ceremony of a most sacred nature, having, as its declared aim, the complete transformation of the person admitted to it. From early times the preparation for it comprised two stages: the catechumenate and the election. The catechumenate was a period of instruction during which the converts were taught their essential duties, as regards the doctrines they must believe and the moral virtues they must practice. The catechumens already belonged to Christian society, but they had not the right to be present at the sacred mysteries properly so called and were sent out of the church after the Gospel and the homily. Entry to the catechumenate was marked, even at this early date, by expressive rites: (1) insufflation, (2) the signing with the cross on the forehead, (3) the administering of salt. We should not lose sight of the fact that these rites, like those we shall describe that were used for the election, which followed the catechumenate, are still used

McClure (London: Society for Promoting Christian Knowledge, 1903), 294–342.

in Baptism nowadays, but they seem to have lost part of their significance when Baptism is given to newborn babies, as is customary in countries that have long been Christian.

Insufflation was an early form of exorcism. In a letter written by a Roman deacon to an official in the time of Theodoric, King of the Goths (at the beginning of the sixth century), we find evidence of this rite. and it is clearly stated that it was accompanied by an exorcism "that the Devil may come out and withdraw."

The signing with the cross was performed with the thumb on the forehead of the person to be baptized. Immediately afterward the priest stretched out his hand over the candidate and recited a prayer containing this mention of Satan, "Drive out from him all blindness of heart; break all the bonds which bound him to Satan."

As for the administering of salt, it was preceded by an exorcism of the salt itself, in which was said, among other things: "We therefore pray You, Lord our God, that this creature of salt, in the name of the Holy Trinity, may become a salutary sacrament to put the enemy to flight." Then the salt was placed in the candidate's mouth and prayer said over him. After that he was deemed a catechumen and could receive instruction.

The second stage preparatory to Baptism was much more complicated and the battle waged against Satan far sharper and more prolonged.

When a catechumen was deemed worthy of being admitted to Baptism, he passed from the catechumen class to that of the "elect" or "competent." Every year, at the beginning of Lent, a list was drawn up containing the names of the elect who were to receive Baptism on Easter night. Throughout the whole of Lent they were to be assiduous in their attendance in church, either to be exorcised or to complete their religious instruction and undergo the examination known as "scrutinies."

According to the documents in our possession, and they go back to the seventh century, the sessions dedicated to baptismal preparation were seven in number. Although we do not possess any catechetical texts in Latin comparable with the famous Greek Catecheses of St. Cyril of Jerusalem, we do know that regular courses of instruction were given to the elect; in particular, we possess some sermons to "the competent" by St. Augustine.

In the seventh century, the examinations, or scrutinies, began only in the third week of Lent. At the stational Mass on the Monday after the second Sunday, the first of these meetings was announced from the pulpit for the next day at noon (the sixth hour). But the Devil was not forgotten in this first announcement: "Pray gather together that we may be able to perform the divine mystery by which the Devil and all his pomps and vanities is destroyed and the door of the kingdom of Heaven is opened, with God's help."

At the first scrutiny the elect were enrolled. The men were separated from the women and then the stational Mass began. After the prayer known as the collect and before the lessons, a deacon called the elect, who prostrated themselves in prayer. All answered, "Amen" to this prayer and crossed themselves at a sign from the deacon. Then the exorcisms took place. *Exorcism* always indicates a battle fought directly against the Devil. Each exorcism was a sort of hand-to-hand combat. What should surprise us is the fact that these exorcisms were repeated almost unceasingly until the baptism itself. A cleric charged with the duty of exorcism—formerly an exorcist and later an acolyte—approached the candidates, the men first and then the women, and traced on the brow of each the Sign of the Cross and then stretched out his hands over each of them as a sign of taking possession. But when the first cleric had finished, a second followed and then a third, repeating the same gestures. And each recited a formula of exorcism, in the middle of which this direct apostrophe to the Devil unvaryingly occurred:

> Therefore, accursed Devil, hear the sentence which is passed upon you and do honor to the living true God, and do honor to Jesus Christ, His Son, and to the Holy Spirit; take yourself away from these servants of God, for God and our Lord Jesus Christ have deigned to call them to His holy grace and by the gift of Baptism to benediction. And this sign of the cross which we trace upon their brows you must never dare, accursed Devil, to violate.

It was a long ceremony: after the passing of each exorcist, the elect were required to prostrate themselves and pray. Then a priest approached, repeated the signing with the cross and the laying on of hands and added a prayer. But he addressed only God and did not mention the Devil.

Finally, when all this was completed, and before the reading of the Gospel, the candidates were dismissed. The exorcisms were repeated in the same form and with the same ceremonial on the other days of the scrutinies, except on the seventh. The third scrutiny was of particular importance. On that day the elect were officially instructed in the Gospel, the Apostles' Creed, and the Lord's Prayer. This was known in many countries as the *Traditio Symboli*, but in Rome it was given the even more expressive name of the "Opening of the ears," or the *Effeta*

(*Ephpheta*). Instead of being dismissed after the gradual,[24] the candidates were given the four books of the Gospels, and the opening verses of each of the four were read to them with a suitable commentary. After the Gospels, the *Credo* was explained to them, either in Greek or in Latin at the request of the candidates, and then the Lord's Prayer. This rite of presentation was very imposing. It was the *Traditio legis Christianae* ("Tradition of the Christian Law") as it was sometimes called.

Finally, at the seventh scrutiny, which immediately preceded the baptism, a priest this time, and not an exorcist, pronounced the supreme adjuration against Satan. Thus, the battle for the deliverance of the candidates to Baptism had lasted a full month, but it is at this point that it took on its most moving form. The priest addressed Satan with authority, in the name of Christ:

> You must know, Satan, that you are threatened with penalties, that you are threatened with torments, that you are threatened with the day of judgment, and that that day will be the day of punishment, a day which shall come in the form of a fiery furnace, in which you and all your angels shall suffer eternal death. Therefore, O damned one, do honor to the living and true God, do honor to Jesus Christ, His Son, and to the Holy Spirit, in whose name and by whose virtue I command you to come out and withdraw from this servant of God, whom the Lord our God has deigned this day to call to His holy grace and blessing and to the fount of Baptism, that he may become God's temple, by the water of regeneration, for the remission of all his sins, in the name of our Lord Jesus Christ.

[24] The singing of psalms, alternating with biblical readings. —Ed.

Then followed the ceremony of the *Ephpheta*. With a finger slightly moistened with saliva the priest touched the upper part of the lips and ears of the candidates, saying: "*Ephpheta,* which means: Open in the odor of sweetness. As for you, Devil, take to flight for the judgment of God draws near!"

And that is not all. The strife against Satan reached its critical point. The candidates were required to renounce him and bind themselves to Jesus alone. They were anointed with oil, like athletes about to enter the arena. Then each candidate presented himself to the priest, who asked him three categorical questions: "Do you renounce Satan? And all his works? And all his pomps and vanities?" And to each, the candidate replied aloud: "I do renounce! *Abrenuntio!*"

After this solemn renunciation, the new disciple pronounced the formulary of the Faith (the *Redditio Symboli*), that is, he recited the Creed. At last Baptism could be given. It was preceded by three solemn questions corresponding to the threefold renunciation of Satan: "Do you believe in God the Father Almighty? And do you believe also in Jesus Christ, His only Son, our Lord, who was born and who suffered? And do you also believe in the Holy Spirit, in the holy Church, the remission of sins, and the resurrection of the body?" To each, the candidate answered: "I believe! *Credo!*" Baptism was conferred, Confirmation immediately afterward, and the new Christians received their first Communion during the Mass that followed.

Such was the Roman baptismal rite; but in the Gallican ceremony, which was in use until the liturgies were merged under Charlemagne, as well as in the oriental rites, exactly the same ideas are to be found in similar forms.

Satan's presence in the midst of us, and his dominion over all those who are not baptized, could not be asserted more clearly or more forcibly. The Church is far from forgetting the practices that have come down to her from her origins and which form her most sacred traditions. In all missionary lands, Baptism is conferred on adult converts with ceremonies deriving directly from those we have just described. And in countries of long-standing Christianity it is the general custom, after the solemn Communion that takes place at the completion of the catechism course, to hold a very moving ceremony in the course of which the children, generally age twelve, are led to the font and, touching the Gospels, make what is known as the renewal of baptismal vows with a formula that is more or less the same everywhere and which requires each child to say: "I renounce Satan, his pomps and vanities and his works, and I take Jesus Christ for my master, forever."[25]

What clearly emerges from all this, as we have insisted throughout this chapter, is the certainty that each one of us has an "angel of persecution," that is, a personal devil, corresponding to our guardian angel.

Nevertheless the Church has never held the opinion that the exorcisms in Baptism form the definitive termination of our strife with the Devil. They put an end to his dominion and his rights over us, but not to the providential function assigned to him by God, in the development of our personal "trial." He still remains as the Tempter; he is still there before God as that "accuser" of whose dreadful and even terrifying interventions, made with God's permission, we read here and there in the book of Job. Not only does the greatest virtue and even holiness itself not protect us, or protect anyone, from the assaults of the

[25] This ceremony has been used in France particularly, but for all Catholics there is similar renewal of baptismal vows annually on Easter.

Devil, but there seems to be a law, which has been constantly verified at least since Job, and which lays down that the greater the graces of prayer received from God, the more terrible do the assaults of the Devil become.

Who can tell us more about this than the man who might be called the prince of mystical theology, St. John of the Cross? In his well-known treatise, *The Dark Night of the Soul*, he is categorical on the particular point with which we are concerned, and he comments on a verse from his *Spiritual Canticle*, in which it is said that the soul rises up to God "in darkness and in disguise." Disguised from whom? For him there can be no doubt: from the Devil, the enemy of our salvation and consequently of our sanctity. But it often happens that the graces resulting from prayer do not escape Satan's notice.

Among the cases in which that happens, St. John of the Cross notes the one in which the blessings are communicated by the mediation of the "good angel." And, from his way of expressing it, we gather that in each individual there is, opposite the good angel, a "bad angel" also. Of course, St. John of the Cross does not quote the passage we mentioned previously from *The Shepherd* of Hermas, which in any case would not have been a decisive authority for him, any more than it is for us. This is what he writes:

> For of those favors (of passive or contemplative prayer) which come through a good angel God habitually allows the enemy to have knowledge: partly so that he may do that which he can against them according to the measure of justice and that thus he may not be able to allege with truth that no opportunity is given him for conquering the soul, as he said concerning Job. This would be the case

> if God allowed not a certain equality between the two warriors—namely, the good angels and the bad—when they strive for the soul, so that the victory may be of greater worth and the soul that is victorious and faithful in temptation may be the more abundantly rewarded.[26]

What a number of things a passage like this has to teach us: God has to maintain a certain justice. Well then, would it be any less just on God's part if we were kept away from temptation? Must His most attentive and faithful servants be, in justice, more subject to temptation than other people? Has the Devil a right to invoke, in this connection, and could he legitimately complain if this right were violated?

Here we are brought to the very heart of the problem of the existence of Satan and his cosmic function. It seems that we should understand the matter in the following way: all the rights that creatures hold before God are the fruit of divine justice. God is just, supremely, absolutely, eternally just. He is so even in his punishments. And thus He desires Satan to have rights just as His free creatures have. And what can these rights be? Not to be treated unfavorably in comparison with other free creatures, be they angels or men. There would be a sort of injustice, inequality, partiality on the part of God—all of them unthinkable if all free creatures were not submitted, as Lucifer and his angels had been, to trials proportionate to their aptitudes, strength, and graces. God would be unjust to Satan if everyone else could achieve holiness without effort and without meriting

[26] St. John of the Cross, *Dark Night of the Soul,* Bk. 2, ch. 23, no. 6, in *The Works of St. John of the Cross,* trans. E. Allison Peers (London: Burns, Oates; and Westminster, MD: Newman Press, 1953), 478–479.

it. That is what the God of Luther and Calvin is like. He seems to us unjust in His decree of predestination because He chooses Hell for some and Heaven for others, regardless of their merits or demerits. Such a God appears monstrous to us. And that is the greatest heresy that the Church has found and condemned in the teaching of Luther and of Calvin.

Thank God, it is not so. God holds an equal balance. He had heaped His gifts upon Lucifer. It was equally in the power of Lucifer to deserve Heaven as it was in the power of Michael and his angels, or, according to Genesis, as it was equally in the power of Cain as of Abel. When God bestows His highest spiritual favors by the intermediary of the good angel, to hold an equal balance, he allows the bad angel to be informed of it and lay his plans accordingly.[27]

But it is clear that by putting forward this doctrine, St. John of the Cross sides openly with those who believe that we all have both a good angel and a bad. And then when he goes into detail about the powers of seduction given to the bad angel to test the souls of those favored with the greatest gifts, he gives us to understand that these powers, limited when used against ordinary mortals and what we might call "the small fry" of Christian virtue, in the case of the former become increasingly subtle and preternatural. Then, instead of authentic visions and apparitions, they may encounter the most dangerous illusions and phantasmagoria. Thus, as St. John of the Cross notes, Pharaoh's magicians could vie with Moses and more or less imitate his miracles. What dangers there are in so-called

[27] It is in this sense that we are tempted to interpret Christ's mysterious words, in Luke 22:31: "Simon, Simon, behold, Satan has claimed power over you all, so that he can sift you like wheat." So God listens to Satan!

mystical revelations! St. John of the Cross, with his long experience of them, never ceases to warn us against them. Even if they come from God, he warns us to ignore them because of the doubt that must always exist concerning them, and he tells us to cling to faith alone.

In short, the nearer we climb to God, the greater right Satan has to lay traps on the road leading up to the heights. The next chapter confirms this grave conclusion that we have reached.[28]

[28] It is important to understand that everything we have said here concerning Satan's "rights" is not an attempt to interpret the divine plan. No creature has any rights except by virtue of this plan, which is the fruit of God's infinite wisdom.

Chapter 6

Monks and Demons in the Desert

True servants of God have never doubted the existence and incessant intervention of the Devil in their lives. The Curé d'Ars knew the Devil from personal experience. Toward the end of his life he spoke of him as an "old comrade" of whom he was not afraid but in whom he recognized an irreconcilable adversary. It is true that from his childhood on, or at any rate from the years that he studied with the good Abbé Bailey, he had learned to read the stories of the fathers in the desert. It was to them that he had looked for examples of superhuman mortification and continual contemplation, and he had learned from them of the aggressiveness of Satan and how to repel his attacks.

In some powerful passages, to which we shall later return, Henri-Irénée Marrou stressed the difficulty experienced nowadays by well-informed Christians when confronted with documents dealing with the Fathers in the desert. There is the greater reason, then, for us to give the difficulty extended consideration in this book.

Most readers, "even believers and sympathizers," says Marrou, "are astonished and often shocked by the natural and normal dealings that the worthy monks of Egypt and elsewhere had with these invisible beings"—although I should venture to say that they were not invisible to them! "The historian's first duty," continues Marrou, "is to record the facts: men who lived in the seventh century A.D. believed in angels, good and bad, not only from the strongest and clearest conviction but also by the most concrete personal experience in everyday life; and that is not an overstatement. It seemed just as natural for them to repeat the words of the psalmist: *In conspectu Angelorum psallam Tibi*,[29] as to admire those heroic ascetics who went off into the desert to fight devils."[30]

Especially we should notice that it was a well-vouched-for tradition that the Devil preferred to prowl in the desert. Leviticus had recommended letting loose in the desert the "scapegoat," the symbolical bearer of all Israel's sins, for in the desert dwelt the bad angel named Azazel. In Tobit (8:3), there was a devil who had been driven off by a sacrifice offered by the young Tobias and who had fled toward "the upper part of Egypt." In that case, the anchorites could not have failed to find him there. Jesus Christ Himself had said that when the demon is driven out of a man, he goes off—doubtless to stifle his fury—"into the desert" (Matt. 12:43).

After the many exorcisms performed by the primitive Church, the "desert" could hardly be lacking in devils! In fact, all the stories of monks in the desert tell of struggles with Satan. If, in France, the old legends about St. Martin only mention the tricks that he contrived to play on the Devil, the same thing applies not only to St. Antony the Great, who is considered the

[29] Ps. 137: "Angels for my witnesses, I will sing of thy praise."

[30] Marrou, in *Satan, Études carmélitaines*, 32; Eng. trans., 71.

father of monks, after the legendary St. Paul, the "First Hermit," but also, as we shall see, to all the other hermits and cenobites in succeeding ages.

∞

There is extant a life of St. Antony written shortly after his death by St. Athanasius, bishop of Alexandria, one of the greatest writers of that century and a leading champion of Catholic orthodoxy against the Arian heresy. The date usually attributed to this biography is 357, while St. Antony died in 355 or 356. Thus, it is a document of the utmost importance. In it there is mention of almost continuous strife between Antony and the Devil. In St. Athanasius's book Antony speaks about Satan as someone he knows very well, although that is to put it mildly, for the whole of Antony's life had been one long battle against him.

From the very earliest years of his solitary retreat, "the decision he had taken henceforth to serve God alone was apparently intolerable for the Devil, who is the enemy of all good." So he began to tempt Antony in every way imaginable. At first he reminded him of the joys he had given up, the sister he had left behind in the world, friends and relatives he would like to see again, the good meals he could have, in short, all the pleasures of life of which — in the Devil's opinion — he had deprived himself so foolishly, just to satisfy a capricious desire for holiness, a desire, moreover, difficult to fulfill, for it was questionable whether his body could stand up to it. Would not his health be dangerously undermined? A whole host of thoughts assailed the young recluse to weaken his resolution. And we can say that what happened to Antony up to this point was exactly what will happen, until the end of time, to all who try to give themselves to God.

After these first assaults, which Antony repelled by prayer and by clinging to God, the Devil set about attacking him at another point which, as the biographer points out, is the most easily accessible in the case of a young person. The higher this valiant Antony rose in virtue, the more the Devil tempted him. He disturbed his nights with lascivious imaginings. He attacked him—with God's permission, evidently, as in the case of that saintly man Job—with such infestations—the word used by Athanasius—that those who witnessed it in broad daylight were convinced it was a real hand-to-hand struggle.

The Devil conjured up obscene visions, and Antony drove him back by prayer. Satan tormented him in his flesh. The young hermit, blushing for shame, fortified his spirit with acts of faith, supplication, and penance. The foul adversary—we are here translating almost word for word—would at night assume the face of a woman and imitate her gestures to deceive and conquer Antony. But he, immersing himself in the memory of Christ and the lofty thoughts of the virtue He demands of us, succeeded in extinguishing the burning coals of this illusion.

"And that is how," concludes Athanasius, "he who believed himself capable of being the equal with God—Satan—was outplayed by an adolescent, and he who prided himself in being so superior to flesh and blood was defeated by a man of flesh and blood who knew, however, that he must lean on the Lord, for the Lord had taken on flesh for love of us and precisely that He might make the body victorious over the Devil. But like all those who struggle, he could say: 'It is not I, but the grace of God working with me!'"

Still with God's permission, evidently, but a permission that extended unceasingly to fresh diabolical assaults, as in the case of Job, Satan, in a fit of rage, appeared in the form of a child. And he held the following conversation with him:

> "I have deceived many, I have conquered a great number, but now, coming against you as against the others, I have proved to be the weaker."
>
> "Who are you then, who speak thus to me?"
>
> "I am," said the other in tones of lamentation, "a friend of lust. I am skilled in tormenting and overthrowing young people by my snares. I am called the spirit of fornication! How many have I deceived of those who wished to live in chastity!... It is I who have so often sought to drag you down and who have so often been repelled by you!"

We may suppose that he was trying by these admissions to make Antony fall into vainglory, into a sin of presumptuousness and pride.

"If that is so," answered Antony simply, "you deserve nothing but contempt; for you are only an impotent child and your soul is black. Therefore I have nothing more to fear from you. With the Lord at my side to aid me, I shall yet see my enemies baffled" (Ps. 117:7).

Antony's biography contains a great number of features of this kind. With Antony, the diabolical infestations often took on forms similar to those described with conclusive evidence by the biographers of the Curé d'Ars. Sometimes the Devil would make such a din that the walls of the place where Antony lived seemed to be caving in. Then devils would rise up on all sides in the shape of various wild beasts and reptiles. Sometimes the hermit seemed to be surrounded by specters. He saw all around him "lions, bears, leopards, bulls, snakes, asps, scorpions, and wolves." Each animal was howling or roaring and seemed to be trying to attack him, according to its nature. But Antony, although undergoing great physical suffering, remained undefeated and unshaken and even had the courage to mock his enemies, just as the Curé d'Ars, who had been brought up under the same discipline, was to do fifteen hundred years later:

"If you had any power at all," said Antony, "one of you alone would be enough to overthrow me. But as the Lord has taken away your power you are trying to frighten me by sheer weight of numbers! This way you have of assuming the shapes of wild beasts is clear proof of your impotence! Attack me if you can, don't hesitate! But if you cannot, why trouble yourselves in vain? I put my trust in the Lord; He is my shield and my rampart."

Each time, the demons seemed to grind their teeth as if they saw it was they themselves and not Antony who were the real victims of these useless attacks!

All these conflicts related by St. Athanasius and famous afterward throughout Christendom were to light the way down the centuries for generations of monks and saints. For what Athanasius tells us of Antony has also happened to many others, especially to saints:

> The Lord, not forgetting Antony in his hour of battle, came to his aid. Then raising his eyes, Antony saw what seemed to be an opening in the roof, through which shone down a beam of light. Suddenly the demons vanished, the hermit's bodily suffering ceased, and his dwelling became whole again. Then St. Antony drew deep breaths and was relieved from all his pain. And he called out to him who had brought him help and said: "Where

are you? Why did you not come at once? Why did you not relieve my sufferings straight away?..."

"I was there, Antony," answered a voice, "and I was waiting and watching your battle! And as you have faced your enemy and emerged victorious, I shall always be by your side and shall make your name famous throughout the world...."

On hearing this, he rose and began to pray, and he felt a power coursing into his limbs far greater than any he had known before. He was then about thirty-five years old.[31]

∞

As Antony died, so tradition tells us, at the age of 105, it is evident that he had still plenty of time to do battle with the Devil and to become fully acquainted with demoniacal theology. So we shall ask him to tell us about this theology, still quoting from Athanasius, who by transcribing it gave it, in a manner of speaking, his episcopal blessing.

He quotes Antony as making the following observations:

> Above all, you must know that if devils are called devils it is not because they were created so. God has never done wrong. Even they were created good and then falling from heavenly wisdom were cast down upon earth. It is they who led the pagans astray with their deceptions. They are consumed with envy of us Christians. They strive with all their might to close the gates of heaven to us and to prevent us from entering, for they have

[31] Migne, *PG* 26, col. 845ff.

been cast out. We must therefore battle against them with prayer and good works and learn, with the help of the Holy Ghost and the discernment of our minds, to distinguish which among them are less evil and which are more so, and how to set about fighting them, and by what means we may drive them off and cast them out.

For they know many and various tricks and go to great pains to catch us in their traps.

If, therefore, they see Christians in general and monks in particular toiling and making great progress, they hasten to assault them and tempt them. They place obstacles in their path, that is, put evil thoughts in their heads. But we must not be frightened by their suggestions. By prayer, by fasting, and by trust in God they may be driven off immediately. But even when they have been repulsed, they do not leave us in peace. They come back to the attack with great violence and skill. When they cannot lead a man astray with obscene desires, they attack him at another point and seek to frighten him with deluding apparitions and, if need be, assume a variety of shapes—the shapes of women, wild beasts, serpents, gigantic bodies, or troops of soldiers. But we must not be afraid of these either, for they are only apparitions and vanish as soon as we fortify ourselves with faith and make the Sign of the Cross.

But they are cunning and ever ready to conceal their true nature beneath all sorts of shapes and masks. They often seem to be singing psalms without showing themselves and repeat words from the Scriptures. At other times, when we are reading, they repeat the words we read like an echo. When we are asleep they summon us to prayer, and often do this just to prevent us from sleeping. Sometimes they put on a monk's habit and utter pious words so that they may deceive by outward appearance and lead astray those whom they deceive. But we must not listen to them, even if they exhort us to pray or advise us to fast; and above all we must ignore them when they seem to be accusing us or abusing us for the faults we know we have committed. Of course, they do not do that in the interests of piety or truth, but simply to discourage the unwary and reduce them to despair by trying to show them that an ascetical life is useless and by making them weary of monastic life with its duties, which they show to be arduous, distasteful, and unprofitable for those who dedicate themselves to it.

But the demons are powerless. They are merely making a pretense like actors on the stage and are trying to frighten the young with their deluding apparitions, their noise, and their disguises. For this very reason we must treat them with contempt, for they have no power. When the Lord sent out an angel against the Assyrians, He had no need of tumult or outward manifestations or of noise or acclamation, but with calm strength He smote down 185,000 men with a single blow (4 Kings [2 Kings] 19:35).

But the less power demons have, the more do they try with empty apparitions to strike terror in the hearts of men.

The more they attempt to do this, the more we should practice all the works of an austere life. The strongest weapon to use against them is pure living and trust in God. What they dread above all are the fastings of

> ascetics, vigils, prayers, gentleness, peace, contempt for money and vainglory, humility, love of the poor, almsgiving, meekness, and above all else, devotion to Christ.

The great anchorite, having expressed these wise and weighty opinions, passed on to a most important exposition of the rules for the discernment of spirits. He was touching upon one of the most delicate points of ascetical and mystical theology.

Since Antony warned his disciples against the wiles of the Devil and mentioned as being particularly dangerous their apparition in the shape of monks and their pious orations, it became necessary to show how to distinguish between a devil in disguise and a real monk, between a good influence and a bad. The Devil exhorts men to do without sleep in order to pray, but a good angel may also encourage us to "watch and pray," as Jesus said to His disciples. It is difficult not to be misled when faced with two cases bearing such a resemblance to one another. To guide us, Antony lays down principles that are simple, logical, sound, and easy to remember: a good influence, or rather, a good angel can be recognized by this characteristic: his intervention leaves the soul in a state of peace. The Lord, through His messengers, fills our hearts with pleasant feelings, with joy, and with a fullness which it is impossible not to feel—the sure signs of the divine presence. That inward light, those words we hear spoken in the depths of the soul: "Be not afraid!" as Gabriel said to Zechariah and as an angel said to the holy women at the sepulcher, are what really prove that an inspiration comes from God.

On the other hand, diabolical interventions are always accompanied by agitation, inner turmoil, unrest, ambitious yearnings, sadness, fears, discouragement, and an inexplicable feeling of weariness.

These were the rules that Antony laid down, but above all he insisted on faith. Never be afraid of the Devil when you have the honor to belong to Christ—such was his unquestionable axiom. And he gave his disciples a proof obtained from personal experience: "One day," he said, "when I was in the monastery, someone came to my door. So I went out and saw a very tall figure, and I asked him his name. 'I am Satan,' he answered. 'And why have you come here?' I asked. And he answered: 'Why do you monks and Christians accuse me wrongfully? Why do you always heap curses upon my head?' And I said: 'But why do you attack us?' To which he replied: 'It is not I who attack you, but you who torment yourselves for I have grown exceedingly weak. Have you not read in the psalm: "Spent is the enemy's power, doomed to everlasting ruin; the memory of them has died with the fall of their cities" [Ps. 9:6]? There is no place of refuge left for me, no weapon, no city. The whole world has become Christian and the deserts are filled with monks. Let them, therefore, look to themselves and cease heaping their curses upon my head.'

"Then it was," concluded Antony, "that I marveled at the grace of the Lord, and I answered him: 'Although you were ever a liar and never speak the truth, this time at least, you have been forced to pay homage to the truth in spite of yourself. Through His coming, Christ has made you weak and taken away your power....' But as soon as I spoke the Lord's name, the Devil could no longer bear to hear me and vanished."

Stories of this kind were ideally suited to inspire men with confidence, and they were handed down the ages. Even in modern times they can be heard from the lips of a man like the Curé d'Ars. This assurance was, of course, far more commendable than the almost complete silence with which too many modern preachers treat the Devil, his power, and even his existence. But this point will be dealt with at the conclusion of this book.

St. Antony's remarks, as related by St. Athanasius, have been fully quoted here because we find in them the real substance of all the experiences, reflections, conclusions, and rules for conduct that should be laid down for the practice of an ascetical life in monasteries. This maxim especially may be drawn from them: diabolical temptation forms part of the law according to which every human being endowed with intelligence and freedom must undergo a trial, a test. And this temptation varies according to the degree of virtue in each of us: for great saints, great temptations. For humbler spirits, temptations fitting to their stature. There is a strict "proportion of justice," as St. John of the Cross said, in the temptation of human beings, just as there was in the temptation of angels. Satan can no longer complain that he has been treated more severely than others. Divine justice permeated with love rules the world.

It would be absolutely wrong, moreover, to think that what has been said of monks and devils in the wilderness—and volumes could be written about this—is valueless and has no application to our daily lives. On the contrary, no one can escape the law of temptation. The struggle between Satan and Christ is the dominant factor in the whole history of mankind, and it is in relation to this struggle, directly or indirectly, that all other events must be considered. Such at least was the exalted philosophy of that tremendous thinker St. Augustine in his famous book *The City of God*.

Chapter 7

Satanism

Although Christ's reign has made tremendous progress in the world and to that extent has driven back the dominion of Satan, nevertheless it has not entirely destroyed it. There exist histories of the Church that tell of the vicissitudes of Christian development, but there is no known history of Satanism. Possibly such a book would be as exciting as it was terrifying. It is true that the history of the Church is simply the reverse side, or the reversal, of Satanism. If St. John the Evangelist was right in saying that the reason for the coming of Christ in the flesh was to undo what the Devil had done, it is impossible to write the history of the Church, from its origin with Adam down to our times, without writing, by implication, so to say, the history of Satanism.

Since we are writing a book in order to answer the very urgent question, *Who is Satan?*, logic dictates that we should give a sketch of what might be termed a history of Satanism.

Three distinct things may be understood by the word *Satanism:* 1. Satan's dominion over the world; 2. the worship of Satan by heretical groups; 3. the imitation of Satan in men's behavior toward God.

In the first place, then, Satan's dominion over the world: it has existed and still does. Until the advent of Christianity it was more powerful than anything else, and even all powerful. That is why, as has been shown, Christ, when speaking of Satan, called him "the prince of this world." For the same reason, St. Paul, going further still, once called him "the god of this world."

It was with this usurped title that Satan dared to appear before Christ, when he offered to make Him master of all the kingdoms of the earth if He would fall down and worship him. Satan had no hesitation in saying: "All this belongs to me!" And Jesus did not dispute the fact. He merely made an exception in His own case and said: "The prince of this world is coming to kill me, but he has no hold over me" (John 14:30). So before Christ, the world as a whole was withdrawn from its one and only creator, the true God. And things have not changed very much since, because this expression "the world" still means all the collective factors opposing the will and the law of God. When we speak of obstacles to be overcome in order to obtain salvation, we invariably follow the example of ascetical writers and point to the Devil and the world, standing, so to speak, shoulder to shoulder.

Satanism, according to this first definition of the word, can be summarized briefly as the principles of the world. It is in this sense that St. Paul contrasts divine with human wisdom. What in the eyes of men is folly — and the Cross of Jesus Christ above all else — is wisdom and strength in the eyes of God.

This dominion that Satan holds over "the world," by which is meant the false principles of worldly wisdom, will endure until the end of time. St. Paul is explicit on this point, and indeed alluding to the end of the world he writes:

> Full completion comes after that, when he [Christ] places his kingship in the hands of God, his Father, having first dispossessed every other sort of rule, authority, and power; his reign, as we know, must continue until he has put all his enemies under his feet, and the last of those enemies to be dispossessed is death. (1 Cor. 15:24–26)

Satan, therefore, is not only king of the fallen angels. He has, of course, his own "angels" which make up the whole army of devils, but he is also king of all men in revolt against God. St. Paul clearly demonstrates this when he writes to the Ephesians:

> He found you dead men; such were your transgressions, such were the sinful ways you lived in. That was when you followed the fashion of this world, when you owned a prince whose domain is in the lower air, that spirit whose influence is still at work among the unbelievers. (Eph. 2:1–2)

St. Paul also, at the beginning of his letter to the Romans, gives a general description of humanity, both Jews and Gentiles, and shows the whole of mankind as subjugated beneath the rule of sin, which for him means the rule of Satan: "Jews and Gentiles," he writes, "as we have before alleged, are alike convicted of sin" (Romans 3:9).

Seen in this light, therefore, a history of Satanism would be a history of the whole human race; it would be a history of errors and crimes, of idolatry and false religions, of hatred and war, of the reign of sin and death, of the road leading to Hell. The Fathers of the Church, observing the close bonds that link all sinners with Satan, had no hesitation in presenting the world as a sort of "mystical body" of Satan. In fact St.

Gregory the Great, echoing the words of St. Augustine, writes: "Undeniably, the Devil is the head of all sinners and they are all members of this head."[32]

By founding the kingdom of God, which is His Church, or rather by completely regenerating this kingdom of God, which had never entirely disappeared from the earth, Christ joins battle against the kingdom of Satan. The two kingdoms are so locked in combat with one another that, as has been stated, it is impossible to write the history of one without mention of the other. They are opposed to one another and yet bound together, just as in the physical world are light and darkness or life and death, and in the moral sphere, good and evil. The only aim of Satan's kingdom is to destroy the kingdom of God. Everything opposed to the rights of God is eminently satanic. When our Scriptures wish to describe the work of Christ, they say that He has rescued the chosen of God "from the power of darkness and transferred them to the kingdom of his beloved Son" (Col. 1:13). And the two kingdoms, which share between them all human beings, are not static. There is no question of a *modus vivendi* between them or, as is fashionable to say nowadays, "peaceful coexistence." It is quite useless to claim neutrality in this matter. "Who is not with me is against me," Christ proclaims (Matt. 12:30). And that is a logical conclusion. If God is love, whosoever does not love God with all his might and with all his soul is a stranger to God. A son cannot be neutral toward a father. Neutrality is the worst possible insult, for it adds to hatred an indescribable feeling of contempt.

The two cities, therefore, are hostile to one another all along the line. "One is the City of God, the other is the City of the

[32] St. Gregory the Great, *Homily 16 on the Gospel; Moralia,* 4, 14.

Devil," said St. Augustine. This universal view of beings cannot be denied by the true friends of Jesus Christ. All great theologians and Christian thinkers have returned to it and treated it at length. Behind the backcloth of human history stands a character, invisible but immortal and universal, who personally or by the agency of his angels really is everywhere. But there is one aspect of satanic activity in the world that defies the imagination, namely, his daily intervention in the inner life of human beings—an intervention that is unseen, secret, and silent. And that is perhaps the most important of all, particularly in a period of religious decadence such as ours. This aspect of Satanism is referred to again at the end of this book, but it must be considered here in relation to past centuries.

∞

Apart from the dominion of Satan, which may be described by the generic and all-embracing term *the world*, has there ever been and does there still exist a more direct form of Satanism in the shape of Satan-worship? Perhaps many of our contemporaries, professing to disbelieve in Satan, will deny the possibility of such a cult; it must be emphasized that that is perhaps the greatest danger of modern Satanism.

In any case history has known—and doubtless still knows in more or less secret forms—a genuine worship of Satan. In particular it is quite certain that in ancient times there was a widespread worship of the serpent in Egypt, in the semitic regions of the East, in Delphi—a well-known center of supernatural divination. This serpent-worship spread in two directions: from east to west and from south to north. In the year 1387, the King of Poland had destroyed a great number of serpents that were being worshipped in his states.

This cult also took the form of an organized religion among the *Ophites*, a sect referred to by St. Irenaeus and Tertullian. The *Ophites*, also called *Naassians*, from the Hebrew word *Nahas* which means "serpent," were a branch of the Gnostics of the second century. In the story of the temptation of Adam and Eve they attached particular importance to Satan as the tempter. They had the greatest respect for *gnosis*, or knowledge of good and evil introduced by the Serpent. Their teachings held that the Creator had withheld this vital knowledge from the first man. So, according to these heretics, the Serpent acted as a real liberator of mankind because he taught men to rebel against God.

There are traces of this teaching to be found in the writings of the famous gnostic Marcion, but there was a far more striking affinity between the *Ophites* and the *Cainites* who, according to St. Irenaeus, glorified as heroes all the famous rebels against God—Cain, Esau, and the Sodomites. They paid homage to Korah, but above all to Judas for having freed mankind from Jesus. St. John was probably referring to secret sects more or less similar to these when in the book of Revelation he spoke of the "synagogue of Satan" (Apoc. [Rev.] 2:9).

It would be difficult, if not impossible, to see any connection between these abominable primitive deviations and the Catharist heresy, which developed in such a strange and dangerous way in France in the twelfth and thirteenth centuries.

There is likewise an illegitimate glorification of Satan in all the dualist sects, because the essence of dualism consists in making Satan a sort of rival of God, a second god, as eternal as the first and independent of Him. Manichaeism, whose doctrines we shall not waste time in discussing, was one of the principal forms of this dualism. The *Kephalaia* or "Chapters" of

Mani, the founder of Manichaeism, which were discovered in a Coptic translation in 1931, are categorical on this point. They call Satan "the King or Prince of darkness." But this expression had a very different meaning to that of St. Paul or St. John. According to Mani, this prince was in fact a pre-cosmic, uncreated, omnipotent power who had made the world and who was therefore the equal of God.

By a remarkable inconsistency, however, Mani did not call him God and forbade any real worship of him. In the Manichaean form of confession, it is a grave sin to pay homage to Satan as a divinity or to offer sacrifice to him. This interdiction, however, was not always observed, and just as sects of serpent-worshippers had sprung up among the gnostics, so within the Manichaean sects whose principal groups were the Paulicians, then the Bogomiles, and finally the Catharists (Albigensians) there appeared very secret groups called Luciferians. Among them Satan was worshipped but sometimes under the name of Satanael—the God-Satan—or of Sammael. In the eleventh century, a Byzantine writer, Euthymus Zigabenes, mentions the cult of Satanael among the Bulgarian Bogomiles—the probable ancestors of our Albigensians. According to them Satanael is supposed to have seduced Eve, and therefore it was he and not Adam who begot Cain.

No one can tell by what dark traditions these dangerous aberrations were handed down, either by word of mouth or by the pen, from one little secret group to another, throughout the ages. For example, in the year 1022 a whole chapter of canons from Orleans in France is mentioned as having been burned at the stake because "they worshipped the devil." Strange events of this kind are often mentioned in the early Middle Ages. The celebrated Joachim of Flora, a Calabrian monk who died in

1203 and bore the name of the Universal Doctor, attributes the same misdeeds to the Catharists. A little later, in 1236, the chronicler Matthew Paris mentions the city of Milan as being the refuge of every sort of heresy, and among them he quotes the heresy of the Luciferians.

It is very probably from the Luciferians that the practice of witchcraft—a practice that spread throughout the whole of Christian Europe, particularly from the thirteenth century onward—is derived. It was against the Luciferians that the first German inquisitor, Konrad of Marburg, took up arms with the utmost vigor. This man was the spiritual director of St. Elizabeth of Thuringia.[33] It would appear that the zeal with which he attacked heretics took him beyond the bounds of discretion and justice. He aroused such violent hatred against himself that he was killed, in 1233, not far from Marburg, by certain infuriated noblemen. In Hildesheim, in 1224, even the provost of a Premonstratensian monastery, Henry Minneke, was condemned.

The papacy officially joined in the struggle against Satanism with the bull *Vox in Rama* of Gregory IX, dated June 13, 1233. This bull was addressed to Siegfried, archbishop of Mainz, to Konrad, bishop of Hildesheim, and to Konrad of Marburg. It contained a description, apparently based on reports from German inquisitors, of the horrible initiatory rites required for entrance into the Luciferian sect. At the meetings when these rites took place, Satan is said to have appeared in person. On the other hand, it must be stated that the bishops of the Rhineland accused Konrad of Marburg, after his death, of extorting from the defendants he was prosecuting the confession of crimes that they had never committed.

[33] Also known as Elizabeth of Hungary (1207–1231).

In the famous case of the Templars, at the beginning of the fourteenth century, more or less authentic confessions are known to have been extracted by torture from certain members of the Order. But those are matters that now can never be certainly known and must be classified among the riddles of history.

In any case, Gregory IX, after his bull of 1233, thought it his duty to temper the severity of procedure against the so-called Luciferians. It is possible and even probable that there were among them, and perhaps, later on, among the Templars also, certain wavering, cowardly minds who thought it was clever to "sit on the fence," as we would say, and fortify themselves against the power of Satan, whom they recognized as a harmful force, and not without reason.

Among the Yazidis, Satan is worshipped under the name of Iblis, which means "devil," under the pretext that Satan was cast down only because of his jealous and exclusive love of the pure idea of God. They teach that Iblis, in his worship of pure love, refused any reward. But this hazardous theology maintains that God forgave the fallen archangel, in view of the loftiness of the motives for his rebellion, and handed over to him the government of the world and the administration of the transmigration of souls. He is called Melek Taiiss—the Angel-Peacock—because he recovered his spiritual colors.

In this brief summary of Satanism down the ages the question of witchcraft, which is a popular derivation of magic, should be dealt with at some length here; but we shall discuss only what is absolutely necessary for our purpose—namely, a sketch of the endless history of Satanism in the world.

We know that what distinguishes magic from religion is the claim to have discovered and practiced ceremonies and rites imposing compulsion on the divinity or on superhuman powers.

To a certain extent the sorcerer claims to be on an equal footing with Satan. He thinks that he has the means of making him act, of bending him to his will, of forcing him to use his power to further his own ambitions. Witchcraft, in this sense, undoubtedly existed on a large scale. It is quite different from the cult of Satan because it claims to be, so to speak, a domestication of Satan. Ideas of this sort have produced unbelievable divagations. Great theologians such as Albert the Great, Thomas Aquinas and Duns Scotus have, of course, always held that the real power of sorcerers is confined within very narrow limits. But after their time, demonological literature assumed very terrifying forms. A certain Joseph Nider, a Dominican preacher and writer with a great reputation in his own order, who died in Colmar in 1438, published under the title of *Formicarius* ("The Book of Ants") a treatise on the practice of witchcraft in his day, and it is one of the richest sources available to us by which to penetrate the frightening maze of superstition existing in that century.

The profuse revelations he makes are not necessarily all true, but this book, published in 1437, may well contain a considerable proportion of truth. Nider is above all the writer to be consulted for information concerning the witches' sabbath.

But the two authors best known for descriptions of the evil deeds of witchcraft are Jacob Sprenger and his book *Malleus Maleficorum* (*The Witches' Hammer*), published in 1486, and Henry Institoris, who re-edited and expanded the work in 1489.

Among the great trials of the Inquisition are many concerned with witchcraft. The manual by Sprenger and Institoris, which in its final edition contained four volumes, was the handbook of anti-Satanism in Europe. Twenty-eight editions of it appeared between 1486 and 1600.

After 1600, however, witch hunts were conducted with less ferocity. Urban VIII (1623–1644) advised judges to treat with moderation people accused of the crime of sorcery, and this example was followed in the lay courts in which, previously, severity had been the general rule.

A list of works published during the last few centuries and dealing with demonology would terrify many of our contemporaries. Obsession with diabolical art was much more rife among Protestants, and particularly Lutherans, than among Catholics. Countless statements are to be found in Luther concerning the Devil, his power, his brutality, and his manifestations.

Protests were raised, however, against the exaggerations of demonology. A few names that uphold the honor of humanity must be mentioned here. The Benedictine William Edeline, in the middle of the fifteenth century; the Carmelite de Beetz, in 1486; and John Wier, in 1564, all contributed toward lessening the severity of prosecutions against witchcraft. But it was above all the influence of the Jesuit Adam Tanner (1626) and his disciple Frederic von Spee that succeeded in the fight against the prejudices on which the battle against Satan was founded in those days. As a rule mere soothsayers were not prosecuted, but only sorcerers or witches accused of "casting spells" and harming their fellowmen by their sorcery. Very often the defendants confessed that they had signed a pact with the Devil. To give an idea of the widespread nature of this satanic disease it will suffice to quote the following figures: in Belgium in the Province of Namur alone, between 1500 and 1650, 400 people were found guilty, most of them women. Of this enormous number, 149 were condemned to be burned at the stake, 49 were acquitted, and 96 condemned to banishment or lesser penalties. The sentence passed on 106 of them is not known. But it was not until 1682 that Louis XIV put an end to trials for witchcraft, as a consequence of dreadful scandals. It may be said that the age of witchcraft—its golden age, if the expression may be allowed—came to an end everywhere in the seventeenth century.

The final blow was struck by Scipio Maffei, in his treatise *The Art of Magic Destroyed*, written in Italian and published in 1750.

There are various reasons for believing that Satanism has been kept alive right up to the present time. The most obvious form of it in modern civilization is, of course, neglect of God, the denial of God's rights, and the claim to be able to organize every form of human life, whether individual, family or social, without reference to God. This will be alluded to at the end of this book. Outside of this effective Satanism, does there exist what might be termed an effective Satanism in which Satan is worshipped and rites are performed in his honor? There are reasons for believing that the answer to this question is in the affirmative. There is no doubt that there are at the present time secret societies in whose privacy Satan, identified with "Astral light," is worshipped.

According to rumors that we have been unable to verify, Pius XI is said to have obtained undisputed proof of Hitler's affiliation with a satanical sect. But failing this affiliation, it was perfectly easy to discern in his politics, actions, and ambitions, and in the violence of his deeds, an obvious similarity with the methods used by Satan at all times and a direct inspiration from him who was "a murderer from the first" and the "father of lies."

Among the satanic rites most often mentioned it will be sufficient to refer to the "black mass." What is really satanic in this rite is first and foremost the desire to profane the most sacred of Christian rites. But what must also be stressed is Satan's tendency to "ape" the divine. It has in fact been said that the Devil is simply "he who apes God." "Black masses," therefore, were vile orgies with anti-eucharistic celebrations added, in which a sort of caricature of the Mass was celebrated. Whenever possible an apostate priest was called in for the purpose. The rites of this mass are believed to have resembled the ancient sabbath of medieval witches. The notorious Marquis de Sade, a professed atheist and a worshipper of "nature," the author of appallingly obscene novels who, after a scandalous life interspersed with richly deserved terms of imprisonment, died in 1814, described in his works satanic orgies in which consecrated hosts were used. In *Les Adventuriers du mystère* (1927), F. Boutet mentions "missals of the satanic cult." The great novelist and convert J.-K. Huysmans has described a black mass in *La-Bas* (1899, chap. 19). Huysmans had associated with professed satanists and had at his disposal the writings of an apostate priest named Jean-Antoine Boullan (d. 1893) who had assumed the name of "the sword of God," and whose mission was "to liberate the Roman Catholic Church." These documents were given by Huysmans to his friend Leon Leclaire, who handed them to the Arabic scholar Louis Massignon. In his turn, the latter deposited them in the Vatican Library on July 14, 1930.

No attempt must be made to state exactly what relationships existed in the past, and may still exist, between the various forms of Freemasonry and the ancient satanic religions, but there is no doubt that Masonic meetings have been held, in the course of which the members indulged in eucharistic profanations. In Fribourg, Switzerland, in a vast grotto, there is a chapel of reparation, taking the place of a sanctuary used for satanic rites.

On December 2, 1947, there died in Brighton, England, at the age of over seventy, a certain Aleister Crowley, who was reputed a master of black magic. He was the founder of two periodicals specializing in Satanism: *Gnosis* and *Lucifer*. He had opened a satanic temple in London. Hymns composed by Crowley were sung there, and the titles of these are significant: "Hymn to Pan" "Collects for the Gnostic Mass." Crowley's disciples recited them over their master's tomb, adding the well-known "Hymn to Satan" by Carducci.

On March 29, 1948, the death of Harry Price, a researcher specializing in Satanism and psychical investigation, took place in London. In one of his reports, Price stated: "In all the districts of London, hundreds of men and women of high education and belonging to the best families, worship Satan and pay perpetual homage to him; black magic, witchcraft, the evocation of the devil, these three forms of 'medieval superstition' are practiced nowadays in London on a scale and with a liberty of action unheard of in the Middle Ages."[34]

In this respect, what applied to London must, in all probability, apply to most of the world's great capitals. So there is, throughout the world, a real recrudescence of Satanism, a sort of restoration of Satan's dominion. And that is what is meant by the *actuality of Satan*.[35]

[34] See the article "Satanism" by Antonio Romeo, in the *Enciclopedia cattolica* 11, col. 1953–1961.

[35] L. Cristiani published a book under this title in 1954, Editions du Centurion, Paris.

Chapter 8

Some Cases of Possession

In view of what has been said, it would lead to a false view of the question if too much importance is attached to the cases of diabolical possession discussed in this chapter. The most serious, deplorable, and common form of diabolical possession is that which is voluntary; it consists either in intentionally worshipping Satan and performing satanic ceremonies of the type discussed in the previous chapter, or else occurs unconsciously by an indifference to, and neglect of, all religious faith and all compliance with the obedience due to God; this is discussed in the next chapter.

By this alone is meant the actuality of Satan, and it will be emphasized how alarming and how distressing it is.

Nevertheless there are cases of possession—occurring against the victim's will—which produce a terrifying impression on all who witness them.

Msgr. Cristiani, in his book *The Actuality of Satan*, quoting Alberto Vecchi, reports an astonishing case of possession which happened in the district of Piacenza in Italy. The following cases occurred at an earlier date but may be termed contemporary, in the historians' use of the word, for they did indeed take place in the nineteenth century. We do not imagine that they are the only ones that happened in the course of a whole century, but they are the only examples concerning which any exact information is available.[36]

First of all there is the case of Hélène Poirier. This was examined by three priests belonging to the diocese of Orleans and related by one of them, Canon Champault.[37]

Hélène Poirier was a humble country girl, a laundress by trade. Her life seems to have been one long obsession, and yet she lived to be eighty. In her case obsession was replaced on at least two occasions, and over a period of six years in all, by a real possession. There is, of course, a considerable difference between obsession and possession. In the former the subject is tormented, hunted, disturbed, and persecuted, but it is not possible to discover with any certainty the presence of a spirit separate from that of the victim. But possession commences when this spirit manifests itself clearly by means of the following signs indicated in the rite of exorcism in the Ritual: an inexplicable knowledge of foreign languages that the subject has never studied, a similar knowledge of remote and secret facts to which the subject could not possibly have had access, and the manifestation of obviously superhuman strength.

In Hélène Poirier's case, the longest and most common periods of obsession were hardly any different from the periods of possession properly so called. But she would not resign herself

[36] See J.H. Gruninger, *Le Possédé qui glorifia l'Immaculée* ("The one possessed who glorified the Immaculate"), published by the author.

[37] Published by Téqui, *Une Possédée contemporaine* ("A contemporary case of possession"), 1834–1914.

either to the obsessions or the possessions, and in consequence her life was a real martyrdom, made up of the most incredible series of plaguings, persecutions, and ill-treatment of diabolical origin. Yet twice she was successfully submitted to exorcism by the Church. In the second half of her life there occurred, indeed, somewhat astonishing compensations in the shape of interventions by her guardian angel, the blessed Virgin, and our Lord Himself.

Canon Champault guarantees the veracity of the facts that he relates concerning her. Not only did he have at his disposal detailed testimony from the two other priests of the diocese, but Hélène Poirier was in his service for several years, and he remained in contact with her until she died in 1914. He declares that the Devil often struck the girl in her mother's presence, gave her resounding but invisible blows, kicks, and punches, and even tried to strangle her. For months, her face, arms, and body bore traces of these terrible assaults. At other times, the Devil would hurl her to the ground, appear before her in one or another of the hideous forms that have been described in the authentic history of St. Antony, as related by St. Athanasius, and she would feel his foul breath upon her face or be almost crushed beneath his weight when she was lying on the ground.

Even more ghastly infestations than those experienced by the Curé d'Ars, at roughly the same period, were inflicted upon Hélène. At night the diabolical spirit would shake the curtains around her bed, making them slide up and down the rods and moving them to and fro for hours on end. And all this took place before the eyes of a score of witnesses whose names are given by Canon Champault. Very often Hélène was seized by the hair, hurled from her bed and dragged across her room or even lifted up in the air. Sometimes they found her half-strangled beneath her bed. On another occasion, in the middle of the night, she was seized by the head and carried forty yards away over the roofs of neighboring houses.

Under these conditions, it is difficult to doubt the truth of the obsessions and possessions that occurred in this instance, particularly as the facts bear such a strong resemblance to what happened in all the countless other cases reported down the ages.

∞

Manifestations of the same kind are to be found in the case—a double instance—of the two boys possessed of the Devil at Illfurt in Alsace.

Illfurt is a large market town in the Mulhouse district, in Upper Alsace. The two boys in question were brothers, Thiebault Burner and his younger brother, Joseph. The elder boy was twelve when, in 1864, the two showed symptoms that at first suggested an illness,[38] but abnormal conditions were very soon noticed in the Burner brothers: while lying on their backs they would spin around and around like tops with extraordinary speed; sometimes they were gripped with hunger that nothing could satisfy; their stomachs would swell to enormous size, and

[38] We do not say that it was not also an illness. But as in the Gospel we often find people suffering from an illness who are also suffering from possession, we must be careful to distinguish, in symptoms taken as a whole, what can be attributed to disease and what to the Devil. There is, of course, nothing incompatible between disease and possession. On the contrary, it is in the Devil's interests to hide his attacks and torments under the appearance of an illness.

then it seemed as if a large ball was rolling around and a live animal moving about inside them.[39]

It was soon obvious to all that the Devil had a hand in it. In fact, when the two children were sitting on their wooden chairs, they would suddenly be lifted up in the air by an invisible power. All this happened, moreover, in broad daylight, in the presence of numerous witnesses who were utterly amazed at what they saw. But the signs of possession increased as time went by, and the total duration of possession was five years, from 1864 to 1869. The boys spoke a variety of languages, although they had learned only the dialect of their village. They gave answers in French, English, German, Latin, and even local dialects, to the questions asked them by the exorcists. They displayed an insurmountable aversion for holy objects. They foretold future events and made predictions confirmed by what happened afterward. They had a reply to every question, and their theological knowledge was never at fault.

Naturally, as soon as it was realized what was happening, a report was sent to the Bishop of Strasbourg, who ordered an investigation. At the same time, by order of the prefect, the sub-prefect of Mulhouse ordered a sergeant of the gendarmerie named Werner to bring him an official report on the events in Illfurt.

At first, Werner was no less incredulous than the policemen sent to investigate the events that took place at La Salette or, shortly afterward, in Lourdes in connection with the appearance of the Blessed Virgin. But he was soon convinced of the

[39] All this was related by P. Sutter, parish priest of Wickerschwihr (Upper Rhine), in the book *Le Diable dans les Possedes d'Illfurt* ("Cases of diabolical possession in Illfurt"), published by Brunet, Arras.

abnormal nature of the phenomena and felt himself obliged to send in a written report to that effect.

Finally, the ecclesiastical authorities decided that there were grounds for carrying out exorcism. As is well known, authorization for this is granted only with the utmost caution. The exorcism took place near Strasbourg in 1869. The devil was called upon to speak his name, and it was discovered that each of the boys was possessed of at least two devils: the elder by Ypes and Orobas, and the younger by Zololethiel and another whose name they did not succeed in distinguishing.

For the exorcism, they put Thiebault Burner into an iron jacket and bound him to an armchair that three powerful men held down with all their strength. But the devil lifted the chair up into the air with the young man, who was then seventeen, violently pushing away the three men and knocking them over. The exorcist had to repeat the ceremony several times before casting out the devils, and this was eventually accomplished by invoking the Immaculate Conception. After the exorcism the two boys became normal once more and their "disease" disappeared, never to return. It is not possible to explain the significance of these "names" assumed by the devils, but there is something very strange and grotesque about the sound of them. The same may be said of the devil Isacaron, by whom Antoine Gay was possessed.

∞

Concerning Antoine Gay, who was born in 1790 and died in 1871, there is a considerable number of authentic documents. We shall confine our account to the salient facts of the case.

Antoine Gay was born at Lanteney (Ain), and in his early youth he learned the carpenter's trade, at which he became proficient. After his military service he settled in Lyon. "He was a handsome man, tall, with brown hair, a pleasant face and regular features." Of a devout inclination, he felt a desire to be a priest. He was then thirty years of age, but he did not achieve his aim until 1836, when he entered the Trappist monastery at Aiguebelle. Soon, however, he was affected by a nervous disorder that obliged him to leave the monastery. As has already been stated, disease is in no way incompatible with possession; on the contrary. Nevertheless in each instance proof must, of course, be given.

Having left the Trappists, Gay returned to Lyon, and here it was that he spent most of his long life. He lived to a great age, for he did not die until 1871, but his whole existence was one long trial, which he bore and overcame with admirable fortitude. He had, close at hand, experts who took an interest in his case, but by the will of God, he was never exorcised, although many requests to this effect were made and even a few abortive attempts to reach a decision. He spent his life as a living witness to the power and maleficence of the Devil, and his courage and resignation never failed him. In this way, Antoine Gay was a real saint. We are, however, taking the word in its modern meaning and have no wish to forestall the decisions of the Church. Some saints traverse the lofty realms of divine mysticism and become sanctified therein, but Antoine Gay seems to have been hallowed by treading the paths the "saintly man Job" trod, that is, by the way of Satanic mysticism.

Informed by Abbé Nicod and Abbé Collet, both priests in Lyon, Cardinal de Bonald, Archbishop of Lyon, asked two doctors to examine Gay. After keeping him under observation for four months, they both came to the conclusion that he was possessed of the Devil. The authentic certificate submitted by

Doctor Pictet and dated November 12, 1843, makes interesting reading.

> I the undersigned Doctor of medicine, residing at La Croix-Rousse, certify that M. Gay was sent to me for examination by M. l'Abbé Collet and by M. Nicod, parish priest of this town, in accordance with the wishes of Msgr. the Cardinal-Archbishop of Lyon for him to be medically examined. Having done this with the utmost care over a period of four months, seeing him daily and at all times and in every circumstance, such as in church, during Mass or at the Stations of the Cross, in both public and private conversation with him, at meals or out walking, etc., I have found not the slightest physical or moral defect in him. On the contrary, I have found he enjoys perfect health both of body and mind. His judgment is sound, and his intelligence, which is well above average, never shows the slightest deterioration even during the extraordinary and unexpected attacks from which he suffers. These attacks, due to some occult cause which medical science is naturally unable to diagnose, motivate bodily activity and speech quite independent from the patient's will.
>
> I declare, moreover, that having joined with M. Gay in prayer and complete mortification of self, my knowledge and my own reason, to beseech the Holy Ghost to come to our aid, I am fully convinced that this extraordinary condition can only be a case of possession. And my conviction is the stronger because during my first private interview with M. Gay, the spirit who speaks through his lips penetrated the very depths of my conscience, told

> me the story of my life from the age of twelve and gave details concerning me which are known only to God, my confessor, and myself. And I testify also that the same thing happened to other people, several of whom have been converted.
>
> (Signed) Pictet, Doctor

Obviously this first examination was not considered sufficient. The case of Antoine Gay was examined, discussed, and investigated from every point of view. Particular importance was naturally attached to the discovery of theological proofs of possession.

The whole problem depends on this one point: is there in this case a spirit independent of Antoine Gay's?

Once again, textual quotation is necessary. At the request of Msgr. Ginoulhac, Bishop of Grenoble, Fr. Burnoud, formerly superior of the Missionaries of La Salette, made a report from which the following passage is quoted.

> In three sessions lasting from one to two hours we conducted an examination of M. Gay, of Lyon. In our opinion it is highly probable that this man is possessed of the devil. Our opinion is based on the following facts:
>
> 1. Because he revealed several secret matters to us that he was not in a position to know;
>
> 2. Because he showed outward signs of displeasure when we recited certain formulae and prayers from the Latin Ritual. As it is undisputed that Gay knows no Latin, we can only attribute to the presence of a superior intelligence the contortions which, having due regard for the circumstances in which they occurred, showed an element of the supernatural;

> 3. Because certain of the replies to questions we asked him in Latin appeared to indicate a knowledge of this language on the part of the spirit who answered us in French through the lips of Antoine Gay;
>
> 4. Because of the numerous testimonials handed to us by trustworthy persons of good standing who all vouch for the good faith, the virtue, and the sincerity of M. Gay. If this testimony be true, then Gay is not acting a part. Assuming this, he is possessed of a devil....

A little later, the same investigator, who by then had become Archpriest of Vinay (Isere), declared that after thoroughly examining M. Gay he was firmly convinced that he was genuinely possessed.

∞

But one of the most extraordinary features of this case lies in the resemblance it bears to the cases of possession described in the Gospel. It has in fact already been mentioned that devils proclaimed in a loud voice that Jesus was the Christ of God. They were obliged to bear witness to divine truth. The devil by which Gay was possessed, who called himself Isacaron, repeatedly declared that he wept with rage at being forced to admit through the mouth of his victim the truths of Christ's religion and to give either wise counsels or proofs of possession.

"The cruellest punishment that God can inflict upon me," he said, "is to force me to undo what I have done."

It will be noticed, in the foregoing remarks, that Isacaron was driven almost demented at being obliged to "give proofs of possession." The attitude of mind of that period should be taken into account. All this took place in the middle of the nineteenth century, at a time when the Devil's tactics were to remain incognito at all costs, to make people ignore him and believe that he does not exist and that everything that had been said about him in the past was pure legend and imagination. People of this period thought themselves too enlightened to believe in the Devil. Men living in the Middle Ages may have believed in him, but the intelligence of this century had driven away these childish notions forever.

Baudelaire's famous saying is often quoted in this context: "The devil's most cunning trick is to persuade us that he does not exist." For indeed it was at this very time that there occurred the cases of possession mentioned in this chapter, and this was perhaps an answer to contemporary unbelief, as were the appearances of our Lady to Bernadette in the grotto of Massabielle.

What was really extraordinary about Antoine Gay's case and what made it a most unusual possession was that the devil, using Gay as his interpreter, not only revealed his presence by shouting, blaspheming, hurling himself about, and writhing in the most unbelievable manner, but also was forced to "proclaim unceasingly—while all this was going on—the glory of the Most High, to sing His praises, to glorify the blessed Virgin, and to laud St. Joseph and the faithful angels."

Nothing of this sort happened in the case of Hélène Poirier, nor of the two boys of Illfurt. In their case the infernal spirit throws itself about, shouts, curses, howls, wails, and blasphemes, but does not preach. Only once the devil—or devils—of Illfurt were constrained to acknowledge the truth of Catholic doctrine and the teachings of Jesus Christ. In addition, these devils never show signs of wishing to leave the body they are possessing. The same thing is not true of Isacaron, the devil who "possessed" Antoine Gay. Time and again he refers to the exceptional part he is called upon to play:

"I am forced to praise You, Sovereign Master," he cries. "All creatures must acknowledge You, Your power and Your goodness, but also Your terrible justice."

"It is I, Isacaron, prince of the devils of impurity, who am forced, by order of him who is all things, to cause many things to be set down in writing."

"Must I, who hate to let men slip from my grasp, serve them as an instrument of teaching!"

"I am obliged to say things which seem to amaze the wisest of men! This do I say to the glory of the Almighty and to the shame and confusion of all Hell!"

"The will of him in whose presence all beings in Heaven bend the knee is that I, Isacaron, who possess the body of Antoine Gay, should speak with his lips, cause his limbs to move, make horrible grimaces appear upon his face and utter frightful cries, I who am daily forced by God to give proofs that men are truly possessed!"

"Oh! Great Master, how You make me suffer; You force me to destroy my fortresses and my ramparts. Cursed be the hour when I entered this body. Never would I have believed that I would be forced to toil for the glory of the Most High and to convert men."

Such are the frequent utterances of this devil. And there is a strong resemblance between the words he uses and those of the possessed mentioned in the Gospel. Moreover he, the father of lies, is obliged to pay homage to truth and in particular to the supreme virtue of certain priests of this time.

Once Fr. de Ravignan, the famous Notre-Dame preacher, was mentioned in his presence:

"He is a man," cried the Devil, "he is a priest! You will ask him to say a Mass for the deliverance of the man possessed, and that my power over him may be taken away before he is delivered!"

When he reveals his knowledge of what goes on inside men's minds, he fully realizes that he is working against his own interests and is serving God by converting sinners. Numerous examples of this could be quoted. Abbé Collet, the headmaster of an educational establishment in Lyon, who took an interest in Antoine Gay, wrote about this one day to the abbot of the Trappist monastery at Aiguebelle: "A great number of people have told me that their sins were clearly revealed to them, in secret, by Antoine Gay. His presence among our orphans has done much to rekindle their faith and devotion."

Abbé Cellier, chaplain to the Brothers at the Maison Ste.-Marie, at Privas, testifies to the same thing.

"Isacaron's utterances," writes Fr. Chiron to the Bishop of Clermont-Ferrand, "have often caused tears to be shed and effected many conversions." And he added: "There is nothing that devils dread more than prayer and meditation. It is a terrible torture to Isacaron when he is forced to make his victim meditate. He also fears the scourge, an instrument of penance whose blows he feels keenly. Penance and mortification greatly reduce his power and his arrogance. He has no fear of learned men if they are not humble, and he defies the erudite to nonplus him with any questions they may put."

It is impossible to include all the details of this memorable case of possession, but we will end this chapter by relating one episode in the long battle that raged around Antoine Gay. He had been taken to Ars. At this time it was not easy to see the holy Curé who was besieged by countless penitents who had come from all over France. On several occasions, however, he was brought before the holy confessor, who knew so well, from personal experience, all the torments with which, by God's permission, the Devil can "infest" a soul. One evening, when priest and penitent were both together in the humble room visited by all pilgrims to Ars, Isacaron brutally hurled Antoine Gay down at the Curé's feet and, shaking his fist at him, said: "Vianney, you are a thief! You snatch away from us the souls of those whom we are at such pains to seduce!"

And this cry of impotent fury bears such a strong resemblance to what the "Grappin"—as the Curé called the Devil—said when addressing the worthy parish priest. But this time the latter made the Sign of the Cross over the victim's head, and the devil was heard to utter a cry of pain and rage.

Chapter 9

Satan and Ourselves

What in this age is our position regarding Satan? Has the tremendous progress made in recent years by scientific discoveries affected our position? In the *Études carmélitaines* volume dealing with Satan, published in 1948, no less an authority than Henri-Irene Marrou speaks out to advise us seriously to examine our consciences in this respect. In his opinion, belief in the Devil has for some time been undergoing a more or less complete eclipse in the minds of the ordinary rank and file of Christians.

Apart from professional theologians, professors whose habit it is to plod through the encyclopedia of dogma with steady and methodical steps, and apart from those privileged souls who are so far advanced in the way of perfection and the life of the spirit that they know every aspect of it, one might say by experiment, I am certain that among the Christians of our day there are very few who *believe* really and effectively in the Devil; for whom this article of faith is an active element of their religious life.

Even among those who say they are and think they are and want to be faithful to the Church's teaching, we discover many who have no difficulty in acknowledging that they do not accept the existence of Satan. Others agree to it only on condition that they be allowed to interpret this belief symbolically, to identify the Devil with evil (with the evil powers, with sin, with the perverse twist in our fallen nature), to which they give a sort of independent existence, detached from any real personality. Most people just find the theme embarrassing—you have only to look at the oratorical precautions that are taken before it is introduced, even by authors with the highest motives.[40]

Belief in the Devil has, therefore, suffered a "regression." Perhaps it is true to say that most intelligent Catholics are unwilling to face up to this article of their Faith, or if they think of it, they inwardly take refuge behind a nebulous interpretation of it. M. Marrou has accurately analyzed their attitude when he says that for many people Satan is simply a personification of evil, a figure of speech, a prosopopoeia. And this attitude has the serious disadvantage of misrepresenting the nature of the moral struggle which is the basis of human life here on earth. We are fighting, or so we imagine, against abstractions that, although seeming very real to us, appear only to be static adversaries, and not intelligent, cunning, spiteful enemies eager to destroy us, and we must call on God, the good angels, and the saints for help to overcome them.

Under a pretext of realism that enables us to refuse acceptance of what we hold to be old-fashioned prejudices, we are forsaking authentic realism. We take no further part in the divinely planned gigantic struggle which, before man was born, took place between the faithful angels and the rebels and still continues on earth with the battle between the righteous and

[40] Marrou, *Satan*, 28–29; Eng. trans., 67–68.

the wicked. And then we are denying ourselves a clear understanding of Original Sin. We are obliged to admit that there are perverse tendencies deep down within our nature, but we no longer remember their origin and no longer connect them with the Serpent's temptation of Eve. In short the whole spiritual combat takes on a different aspect as it loses its clear outline in the gray shadows of a theoretical argument between our abstract moral principles and our unthinking instincts.

What a distance separates this conception of our testing on earth and St. Paul's interpretation of it in the already quoted passage: "It is not against flesh and blood that we enter the lists; we have to do with princedoms and powers, with those who have mastery of the world in these dark days, with malign influences in an order higher than ours." (Eph. 6:12).

Which way does true realism lie? Is it to be found in watering down or even suppressing those truths that have reached us by divine revelation and mystical experience down the ages, or must it be sought in the Faith taught by the Church ever since her foundation?

As M. Marrou so rightly adds, "When the Fathers affirmed the existence of angels and devils and put forth opinions on their nature, there can be no doubt but that they considered themselves to be not merely setting down an act of faith but contributing to a science—a human science based on reason and experience. They spoke of demons as we today speak of evolution, as fact, or rather as a hypothesis accepted without argument by every educated mind.... Yet within this framework borrowed from the culture of their time, the Doctors of the early Church teach us something of true revelation."[41]

[41] Ibid., 35–36; Eng. trans., 74–75.

There can be no doubt that it is a dangerous minimization of the conditions of the Christian combat and a modification of the outlook of our faith, if we underestimate the forces against us, if we forget the presence of the "roaring lion" mentioned by St. Peter, or if we remain within the misty realm of reason while a hand-to-hand, or rather man-to-man, battle is being fought not only within the confines of our individual lives, but also in a great unending war which, first waged in Heaven by the angels, will not cease until the end of our earthly world.

∞

If it is imperative that believers should amend their ideas, if we must return boldly and openly to our Christian tradition in its entirety, there are certain considerations that will help us to understand the present state of the great struggle and urge us even more strongly to this amendment and this return.

Before our very eyes, Satanism has assumed a new shape. In a previous chapter, we saw how Satanism reveals itself in three forms: first, as the domination of the world by Satan, second, as the worship of Satan, and third, as man's emulation of Satan's revolt. It is this third form that nowadays seems the most menacing. The more or less secret chapels in London and other great cities of the world where Satan is worshipped do not represent the real danger. Modern Satanism lies in the neglect of God's rights, in the denial of His name, in the theoretical or practical negation of His existence and authority, and in man's determination to arrange his life apart from God and without God.

Satan can remain hidden in the wings and preserve what has been described as his incognito. He is quite prepared for man to deny him, provided that man also denies God. He who, as the expression goes, "believes in neither God nor the Devil," is just the man for him. This rebellion on the part of man is a second version of the angel's revolt. Satan has found imitators. They are numerous at the present time. And, like him, these "limbs of Satan" take up strategic positions, thereby revealing the attitude of the "father of lies." Perhaps it seemed incomprehensible that angels created by God could have been capable of uttering the blasphemous cry: *Quo non ascendam?*—To what heights shall I not rise?

What madness indeed to consider oneself on a level with God, to prefer oneself to God! Yet that was Satan's sin. But if we read contemporary authors, from the eighteenth-century *Encyclopedistes* to those of the present day, we shall see Satanism clearly at every turn. When mention is made of "the heroic affirmation of Man's Ego defending its absolute integrity," when people boast of "the autonomy of human conscience" or violently denounce all limitations and restrictions of human personality, when men glorify the delights of total liberty and the absolute right of human instinct to develop without restraint, it is nothing else but Satanism.

In practice many, possibly, do not follow out their ideas to their logical conclusion. Their "libertinism" is more in their actions, in the violence of their passions and their self-indulgence than in any considered and conscious doctrine, yet in reality they are living "satanically" because they are living outside God's laws.

It is no doubt seldom that anyone seeks to taste what J.-K. Huysmans termed the forbidden pleasure of transferring to Satan the homage and prayers due to God alone. This taste for blasphemy, this love of irreverence, this quest of the abnormal, by profaning real worship, the abuse of carnal pleasures, accompanied by parodies of Catholic liturgy are a form of Satanism, certainly, but not the most common form, nor that which causes the worst havoc in modern society.

What is more serious, perhaps, is the present-day attitude that revels in knowledge and technical skill, claiming to be sufficient to itself and to humanity and despising all the lofty aspirations that Christ brought into the world. To Christ's words: "How is a man the better for it, if he gains the whole world at the cost of losing his own soul?" this attitude arrogantly replies: "How is a man the better for it, if he saves his soul at the cost of losing the whole world?"

Modern man fosters the ambitions that Prometheus had in antiquity. Modern discoveries have opened up limitless possibilities for him, with the result that widespread among the peoples of the world there is a latent Satanism consisting in expecting everything of science and technical skill and nothing of God, in selling one's share of Paradise for the mess of pottage of material comfort.

∞

Notwithstanding all the denials, the derision, the scorn and the pretence of incredulity, our modern literature is full of allusions to Satan. Among the titles given to their periodicals by the great social agitators of the nineteenth century, Saint-Simon, Enfantin, Karl Marx, Blanqui, Proudhon, and countless others, those most commonly met with are *Satan*, *Lucifer*, *The Antichrist*, *The Atheist*, *The Thief*, *The Ass*, and so forth. The militant atheism of many modern writers, the hatred of God that is one of the aspects of present-day communism, the laicization that banishes God from institutions such as schools and law courts, are clearly all a form of Satanism—that is, a revolt against God, in imitation of Satan.

Satan and Ourselves

There are many writers of our time who, while denying both God and Satan, proclaim Satan's victory over God. In *The Marriage of Heaven and Hell*, William Blake, haunted by apocalyptic visions, was paving the way for Baudelaire's Satanism and singing a hymn to the sacred insurrection of Man against God (1790). After him the prime mover in the exaltation of Satan in literature is Byron, in his *Manfred* (1817), and even more in his *Cain* (1821). In the latter work he makes the murderer of Abel, a sinister man of genius, the victim of his pity for mankind. The poet Shelley, in his turn, sides with Prometheus against Jupiter; that is tantamount to saying with Satan against God.

In recent times it is perhaps Faust, even more than Prometheus, who is taken as the model of a man seeking knowledge and power by means of a pact with Satan. In this connection it would be interesting to study the different interpretations of the Faust legend, for example the version by Goethe, without doubt the greatest of all writers to handle this theme, that of the German novelist Klinger or of the unhappy Lenau, who, like his hero, finally committed suicide. We can take this last writer as an example.

In his poem, dated 1836, his hero, Faust, is searching for the secrets of nature. He can find them neither in the amphitheater of anatomy nor in the chemical laboratories of his time, nor in the mysterious depths of the forest where he pursues his quest. Mephistopheles appears and Faust sells his soul to him, on condition that all his wishes will be granted. He then has all sorts of adventures which leave him weary and disillusioned. Finally he hurls himself down from the top of a rock, and Mephistopheles carries away his soul.

In one form or another, but more often than not without any reference either to God, Satan, or the soul, the contemporary novel is simply a glorification, or at least a realistic, a moral and complacent portrayal, of the worst kinds of sensual aberration. It is still the same Faust in quest of happiness, but he does not seek it close at hand, and he always mistakes the shadow for the substance.

People sometimes quote this saying of the somber Jacob Boehme, a Protestant Theosophist of the seventeenth century (1575–1624): "The devil is nature's cook, without him life would be a bowl of tasteless gruel."

It seems that most modern novelists share this opinion. Their marked taste for filth, their determination to strip man of any lofty ideal, their contempt in dismissing all morality, prove that they are only in their element when painting the most abject vice and that they can count upon the eagerness of their readers to accept the foulest and most pornographic descriptions. And certain publishers, who do good business with this kind of literature, appoint panels of literary experts who are careful to sing the praises of only the vilest books. Writers seem to vie with one another in scatology. Paul Claudel raised his voice in protest against this. And the flood of immoral books devoid of any literary talent which pours into the popular market is even worse, if possible, than those by authors showing some ability as writers and storytellers.

There can be no doubt that these are all written "under the sign of Satan." And Satan has no need to make a personal appearance. He is only too well served by those who profess to believe no longer in his existence or his activity. Denis de Rougemont was quite right, therefore, in confirming Baudelaire's statement: "The devil's first trick is his incognito." This very denial of the Devil on the part of a great number of our contemporaries is the surest sign of their subservience to him.

He is the father of lies, and there is no more deadly lie than the refusal to recognize his presence here in the very heart of human affairs.

∞

Apart from denial of the Devil, we have witnessed pity for the Devil. We need not waste much time in discussing the book by Papini on the Devil, in which he propounds the theory that it is the charitable duty of all Christians to pray for the conversion of Satan, because the punishment inflicted upon Lucifer, which he acknowledges as supremely just, "makes God suffer" just as much as the Devil himself. "Has anyone ever realized," Papini writes, "that this condemnation [of Satan] also condemns God to suffer at the same time? The punishment of Lucifer becomes simultaneously, but in a different form, the punishment of God."

To make such a statement, one would need to have a very poor opinion of God, His immutability, His infinity, His identity with truth, beauty, goodness, holiness, and boundless beatitude.

But Papini was far from being the first to be moved to pity over Satan and his fate. Without going right back to the great Origen, who even when in error wrote with such distinction, we may remember what Victor Hugo learned from the turning tables in Jersey. On December 8, 1853, the spiritualist-poet asked Moses, whose spirit he had conjured up, this question about Satan: "Will his punishment be eternal?" And Moses, who was in a position to know the truth about all things, answered as midnight approached: "All wicked men shall slowly be transfigured and become righteous. The effulgence of God's light shall traverse the vastness of space and melt these icy hearts, and their crimes shall all go hurtling down like a waterfall into the abyss of divine pardon."

Encouraged by these declarations from Moses, Victor Hugo boldly interrogates Jesus Christ, the Moses of the new Law. And on February 11, 1855, Jesus Christ, by the intermediary of the tables, answers by reproaching subsequent Christianity "for teaching love by the name of charity and hatred by the name of Hell." On February 18, Jesus Christ once again speaks out against "the eternal flames of Hell." On March 8, an anonymous spirit proclaims the true gospel, in the following form: "True religion is an immense taming of wild beasts and not an immense stake.... It is a vast feeling of love for all the cruel ones, the infamous and the reviled."[42]

But the "spirits" themselves who spoke to Victor Hugo in Jersey were simply prolonging a campaign to reassess Satan's case. This campaign had already found some illustrious champions.

By 1820, Alfred de Vigny had set the problem in *Eloa*, which, moreover, contained a sequel in which Satan was saved. Lamartine, in *La Chute d'un ange* ("The Fall of an Angel"; 1837), Theophile Gautier, in *Une Larme du Diable* ("The Devil's Tear"; 1839), Soumet, in *La Divine Épopée* ("The Divine Epic"; 1840), and even Victor de Laprade in *Psyche* (1841), had all spoken out in favor of the Outcast.

It was left to Victor Hugo to testify most strongly for him when, characteristically, he raised his mighty voice in his poem *La Fin de Satan* ("The Death of Satan"), written between 1854 and 1860. The brilliant critic Abbé Claudius Grillet found in this uncompleted work "passages of such power and such variety that it must surely be considered as Victor Hugo's masterpiece."[43]

[42] All this is from *Les Tables tournantes de Jersey, Procès-Verbaux* (A record of the turning tables in Jersey)(Paris, 1923).

[43] Claudius Grillet, *Victor Hugo Spirite* (Lyon, 1929), 163.

Like Papini, Victor Hugo contrasted Satan with God himself, as a limitation of God, therefore, in Papini's sense of the word, a "pain" felt by God. It is hardly necessary to say that that seems so absurd that we shall not waste time over it. How childish to attempt to limit the Infinite!

And yet the poet understood that the one condition necessary for Satan's rehabilitation was love. If Satan could only perform an act of love, all would be forgiven. But he will not. His overweening pride opposes it, and this eternal sin explains and justifies, in his case as with all the damned, eternal Hellfire. Therefore, Victor Hugo, in order to make the pardon granted to Satan acceptable to his readers, makes him say:

Ye heavens, azure sky, vast realms of space,
Ye splendours, know that love detesteth me!
No, I hate thee not!

And he concludes thus: "Satan is dead; reborn is Lucifer divine!"

It must be admitted that this vision of Victor Hugo's is indeed a magnificent one, when he makes this prophecy in the *Légende des siècles*:

This shall be God's will. Then suddenly shall strife,
The axe, the block, the gallows and the rope,
The Serpent vile, cast out from heaven, and blood
And cries of hatred, all that's base and foul,
To love and ecstasy transformed be
By one kiss from God.

But he still starts from the same hypothesis: Satan's repentance, Satan's tears: and this explains the heading of his last chapter: "Satan Forgiven."

Victor Hugo felt so certain about this point only because of the revelations of the turning tables in Jersey. On March 8, 1855, the anonymous spirit that spoke to him said: "The Gospel of the past said: the damned; the Gospel of the future shall say: the pardoned."

So he makes it quite clear to us that he means a new gospel. Papini insists upon obedience to the authentic Gospel, that of Jesus Christ, and in this connection he is clearly inferior to Victor Hugo, who knew full well that in Christ's Gospel are the words: "Go far from me, you that are accursed, into that eternal fire which has been prepared for the devil and his angels" (Matt. 25:41). And he must have known that an eternity of sorrow is parallel to an eternity of joy: "And these shall pass on to eternal punishment, and the just to eternal life" (Matt. 25:46).

∞

Whither are we bound now? Terrifying voices try to make us believe that God is dead, that there is no God but man himself. We must read once again the famous passage in which Nietzsche, who was driven mad by it, proclaims this event. He cried:

> Where is God? I will tell you! We have killed him—you and I! We are all of us his murderers! But how have we done it? How have we drunk the Ocean? Who gave us the sponge with which we have wiped away the horizon? What did we do when we detached this earth from its sun? Whither does it go now? Whither are we bound? Far from all the stars? Are we not hurtling downwards now in an endless fall? Backwards, sideways, forwards, in all directions? Is there yet a summit and a base? Do we

> not wander through an infinite void? Can we not feel the breath of limitless space? Is it cold no more? Does not night become yet darker still? Must we not light the lamps in the midst of day? Do you yet not hear the grave-diggers laying God in the earth? Can you yet not smell God's rotting corpse?—For gods also rot away! God is dead! Dead shall God remain! We have killed him. How shall we ever be consoled, we the vilest murderers of all? All that was most sacred and most powerful in the world has bled beneath our knives—who shall wash these bloodstains from our hands? What water cleanse them? What feasts of expiation, what sacred games must we invent? Is not so great an act beyond our power? Must we not become gods ourselves, if only that we may appear worthy of having accomplished it? Never was so tremendous a deed done before, and all those who come after us shall, thereby, belong to a history greater than all that has gone before!

All this was spoken, in Nietzsche's book, by a madman. But what proves that he saw therein at least a prophecy of the future is the fact that he continues thus:

> Then the madman was silent and once again looked at those who were listening to him: they, too, were silent and cast anxious glances upon him. Finally, he hurled the lantern upon the ground and it was broken into fragments and the light was extinguished: "I have come too soon," he cried, "the time is not yet at hand. This tremendous event is still upon its way, it is drawing near but it has not yet reached the ears of man. Lightning and thunder, the light of the stars, great deeds, even after

> they have been accomplished, all need time before they can be seen and heard. This deed is yet more distant from you than the remotest constellations—and yet you have done it!"[44]

Must we conclude this brief survey with an act of defeatism, shaming our Christian Faith? There would be nothing else to do if we accepted the contention of a character created by another great visionary of Nietzsche's day, the great Russian novelist and devout Christian Fyodor Dostoyevsky. In his novel *The Demons*, published in 1867, he makes one of his characters, Shigalev, predict the future of mankind; according to him, this is what should have happened to us by now:

> The old conception of the world, and above all the old morality, will disappear. Men will unite to extract from life every possible kind of pleasure. The human spirit will be puffed up with pride as great as Satan's and man will be deified. Ever triumphant over nature, by his knowledge and his will, man will experience by that very fact, a joy that will replace his hopes of happiness in the world to come. Every man will proudly face his death with calm resignation, as a god would; he will not lament over the brevity of life and will love his brothers with unselfish love.

Such will be the "golden age" also described by Aldous Huxley in *Brave New World*.[45]

[44] Friedrich Nietzsche, *Die frohliche Wissenschaft*.

[45] It seems clear that the Satanism of several of these great writers—Huysmans, Dostoyevsky, Baudelaire, Nietzsche—has a certain quality of despair, regret, and need of God.

It is for readers to say whether such a world seems already to have arrived or whether at least it is on its way. But the author of this book, who throughout has made no secret of his faith, is unwilling to consult the false prophecies of characters in fiction. He will call on the peerless prophet of the book of Revelation to describe for him the last days of the world:

> Then I saw a new heaven, and a new earth. The old heaven, the old earth had vanished, and there was no more sea. And I, John, saw in my vision that holy city which is the new Jerusalem, being sent down by God from heaven, all clothed in readiness, like a bride who has adorned herself to meet her husband. I heard, too, a voice which cried aloud from the throne, Here is God's tabernacle pitched among men; he will dwell with them, and they will be his own people, and he will be among them, their own God. He will wipe away every tear from their eyes, and there will be no more death, no mourning, or cries of distress, no more sorrow; those old things have passed away.

Doubtless this happiness, this real golden age must necessarily be assigned to a life other than that which we know here on earth. But St. John also saw the essential features of the age that will precede this total renewal of all things.

And far from seeing, like Dostoyevsky and Nietzsche, the complete disappearance of the old morality and the "death of God," he comes much closer to the reality that stands before our eyes at this moment, when he writes: "Meanwhile, the wrong-doer must persist in his deeds of wrong, the corrupt in his corruption"—and that is one aspect of our times, but there is another: and St. John continues: "The just man must persist in winning his justification, the holy in his life of holiness" (Apoc. [Rev.] 22:11–12).

So there will always be the two Cities that St. Augustine saw, the two Standards described by St. Ignatius Loyola. But God is not dead! He has nothing to fear from the paltry "Satans" that hover above our heads, here in the midst of mankind. He will have the last word. And this is how St. John describes it:

> Patience, I am coming soon; and with me comes the award I make, repaying each man according to the life he has lived.
>
> I am Alpha, I am Omega, I am before all, I am at the end of all, the beginning of all things and their end. Blessed are those who wash their garments in the blood of the Lamb; so they will have access to the tree which gives life, and find their way through the gates into the city. No room there for prowling dogs, for sorcerers and wantons and murderers and idolaters, for anyone who loves falsehood and lives in it.
>
> The Spirit and my bride [the Church] bid me come; let everyone who hears this read out say, Come. Be it so, then; come, Lord Jesus. (cf. Apoc. [Rev.] 22:12–15, 17–18, 20)

Select Bibliography

Works by non-Catholic writers are marked with an asterisk.

*Baldick, Robert. *The Life of J.-K. Huysmans*. Oxford and New York: Oxford University Press, 1955.

Bruno de Jesus-Marie, O.C.D., ed. *Satan*. London and New York: Sheed and Ward, 1951. (This collection of essays—a translation from the French of the *Études Carmélitaines* volume published in 1948—by various authorities provides an exhaustive treatment of the subject with very full references.)

Kelly, Bernard J. *God, Man and Satan*. Westminster, Md.: Newman Press, 1951.

Thurston, Herbert, S.J. *The Physical Phenomena of Mysticism*, London: Burns & Oates; Chicago: Regnery, 1951.

———*Ghosts and Poltergeists*. London: Burns & Oates, 1953.

———*Surprising Mystics*. London: Burns & Oates; Chicago: Regnery, 1955.

*Waddell, H. *The Desert Fathers*. London: Constable, 1936; New York: Barnes and Noble, 1955.

Wiesinger, Alois. *Occult Phenomena in the Light of Theology*. London: Burns & Oates; Westminster, Md.: Newman Press, 1957.

An Invitation

Reader, the book that you hold in your hands was published by Sophia Institute Press.

Sophia Institute seeks to restore man's knowledge of eternal truth, including man's knowledge of his own nature, his relation to other persons, and his relation to God.

Our press fulfills this mission by offering translations, reprints, and new publications. We offer scholarly as well as popular publications; there are works of fiction along with books that draw from all the arts and sciences of our civilization. These books afford readers a rich source of the enduring wisdom of mankind.

Sophia Institute Press is the publishing arm of the Thomas More College of Liberal Arts and Holy Spirit College. Both colleges are dedicated to providing university-level education in the Western tradition under the guiding light of Catholic teaching.

If you know a young person who might be interested in the ideas found in this book, share it. If you know a young person seeking a college that takes seriously the adventure of learning and the quest for truth, bring our institutions to his attention.

www.SophiaInstitute.com
www.ThomasMoreCollege.edu
www.HolySpiritCollege.org

SOPHIA INSTITUTE PRESS

THE PUBLISHING DIVISION OF